BIG BLUE BLUES

The never-before-told story behind the point-shaving scandal that put a stain on a glorious 1940s Kentucky college basketball era

KEN MINK

2

Copyright 2011

FOREWARD

The history of basketball at the University of Kentucky is filled with national championships, conference titles, coaching records, all-American players and perhaps the most devout fans in the country.

And just a few point-shavers.

Kentucky's involvement in the 1940s-50s college basketball point-shaving scandals has been well-documented. The Wildcat players involved received some harsh punishment and the school itself suffered greatly.

But when one looks at the entire picture of Kentucky's involvement in the scandal a fuller, clearer more definitive story evolves – one that reveals there was minimal involvement by Kentucky players and the punishment handed down for these players and the school arguably seemed excessive. The axiom that the punishment should fit the crime does not seem to have been applied.

In doing research for this book I talked to numerous former UK players, journalists and player relatives. But the gist of my information came from the many hours I spent with the late, great UK basketball coach Adolph Rupp and his assistant, Harry Lancaster, when I covered UK athletics for the Lexington, Ky., Leader newspaper in the early 1960s. I spent numerous hours with Rupp and Lancaster at daily UK hoops practices and in social gatherings away from the court. Coach Rupp, in particular, was constantly regaling me with stories of people, players and incidents involving his 41-year tenure at UK. Many of those stories revolved around the point-shaving scandal and his 1940s-50s teams.

This is a book inspired by true incidents using public domain data, news reports, etc., and is basically factual, with some dialogue based on circumstance probability. Especially useful was statistical data from Jon Scott's bigbluehistory.net web site.

Ken Mink

INDEX

CHAPTER 1

Stars Arise from Humble Beginnings

CHAPTER 2

To Stay and Play or Go Away

CHAPTER 3

First Success, Then Comes the Gamblers

CHAPTER 4

A Point Spread Deal Goes Awry

CHAPTER 5

Cats Boot Gamblers, Win Second NCAA

CHAPTER 6

Fabulous Five Gone: Penalties Await

CHAPTER 7

Point-Shaving Scandal in Full Bloom

CHAPTER 8

Wildcats Again Champs, But Storm Clouds Loom

CHAPTER 9

Punishment Fallout Disastrous

CHAPTER 1:

Stars Arise from Humble Beginnings

Ralph Beard had survived the horrible American Great Depressions of 1929 and 1937, but the economic hardships of those years weighed heavily on him when at the fuzzy-cheeked age of 17 he enrolled at the University of Kentucky on a basketball scholarship in September 1945.

Beard had been too young for the military draft, but World War II had just ended and a lot of athletes were returning to colleges after serving in the U. S. military.

Kentucky was one such team, with several players returning to the Wildcats after finishing their tour of duty.

Beard was assigned to a room in the somewhat austere UK athletic dormitory on Washington Street and arrived there carrying a paper bag with a bologna sandwich inside.

He had learned to be frugal, growing up in a home with a mother who had to work long hours cleaning houses to feed and clothe him and his sister and little brother, Moorman. He also had another younger brother, Frank (who later became a star professional golfer). His parents were divorced and Ralph and his brother, Moorman ("Monie"), lived with their mother while Frank lived with his dad.

As a 10-year-old he had a shoeshine box and walked the streets of Louisville, shining shoes for a nickel.

"Sometimes on weekends I would m-m-make a couple of dollars," he said. "I would take the money home and g-g-give it to my mother."

Beard also had a minor stuttering problem.

"Podnah, most p-p-people don't know what it's like to wonder where their next meal is going to come from," Beard told his freshman dorm roommate Wallace (Wah Wah) Jones.

"Oh, I know alright," said Jones. "There were many kids in our area who never even knew where their next pair of shoes was going to come from. Some of us had to wear cutout cardboard in our shoes when we got holes in them."

Beard and Jones were perfect complements. Jones had grown up in the little Eastern Kentucky coal mining town of Harlan and – like Beard – was a multi-sport star in high school. Jones was considered one of the top high school players in the country, scoring 2,398 points in his four years of high school play.

Like Beard, Jones also came from a broken home. His father and mother, Hugh and Faye Jones, divorced when he was young. The couple had been operating a little Harlan restaurant together. After the divorce, his mother kept the restaurant and the kids.

Wah Wah's family lived in a two-story frame house on the corner of Second and Mound, across from the old Harlan Hospital. His mother rented rooms to boarders and provided them meals. When the cafe went out of business, Wah's mom enlarged the dining space in their home and she called the place The Mound Street Inn, serving lunch and Sunday dinners to the public. Wah Wah spent a lot of time washing dishes, busing tables and helping in the kitchen.

In high school Beard had made all-state as a junior and a senior and was considered by many as perhaps the fastest player in the state. He was an outstanding football and baseball player, as well.

Jones had led his Harlan High Green Hornets to the Kentucky state high school basketball championship in 1944 and Beard had led his Male High Bulldogs to the same title in 1945.

The joy of winning a state championship for Wah Wah was somewhat muted when his team returned from Louisville to find someone had burned down his high school. He had to attend classes at the Harlan Baptist Church the rest of the second semester.

The two had known of each other from their starring roles on their high school basketball, football and baseball teams. Each held a love for their state university and great respect for its legendary coach and decided to cast their lots with Kentucky.

And now they were thrown together, two players destined to become athletic legends.

They both had tremendous athletic hearts and both were driven to succeed in their quest to overcome their relatively impoverished upbringings.

But they differed greatly in physical appearance. Beard was 5-10 and 175 pounds while Jones was 6-4 and 205 pounds.

Beard spent countless hours practicing basketball. His hoops coach at Male High had even instructed the gym janitor to give Beard a key to the gym so he could practice any time he wished. The dynamic Beard could sometimes be found dribbling and shooting away until the wee hours of the morning.

"Are you here to play basketball, football and baseball, like me?" said Jones, lying down on his bed and stretching his arms over his head.

"Oh, yeah, I'm g-g-gonna give 'em all a shot. But I like basketball the best," said Beard, tossing his bag onto his bunk bed. "Would you like h-h-half of my sandwich?"

"Nah, thanks, though. Coach Shively (UK athletic director and interim football coach Bernie Shively) has talked to Coach Rupp (UK basketball coach Adolph Rupp) and they agreed to let me try both football and basketball," said Jones. "They both agreed baseball would be no problem, either."

"Yeah, they told me the s-s-same thing," said Beard. "There's another guy here, John Chambers, who is on all three teams, but they say he is better at baseball than anything."

"Yeah, he tried them all last season, but he was a bust at basketball. He dropped that. But he was very good at football and baseball – he was the team quarterback in football and a pitcher in baseball. They say he has major league baseball talent."

"So, whatta ya think of Coach (Adolph) Rupp," said Beard. "I know he is a great c-c-coach and all but I hear he is sort of a bastard. I met him just once before I signed and he was friendly enough then."

Jones laughed.

"That's what I hear, too. A couple of the guys who are coming back to school from the Army told me Coach Rupp is much tougher than any of the drill sergeants they had. They said you just gotta get used to him, don't let him get under your skin," said Jones.

"By the w-w-way," said Beard, "I never did hear how come you are c-c-called Wah Wah. How did that happen?"

"When I was young I had a little sister named Jackie. When she was first learning to talk she couldn't say 'Wallace' – it kept coming out 'Wah Wah' and so that's what everybody started calling me."

Jones had a fabulous high school career, averaging about 30 points a game as a senior – scoring 69 in one game alone.

Among the UK basketballers who served in the Army and returned to UK were Cliff Barker, Ken Rollins, Jack Parkinson, Bob Brannum and Joe Holland.

Barker had left Kentucky after his freshman year to serve in the Army Air Force. He became a gunner in a B-17 bomber. His plane was shot down and he bailed out over Germany and was held as a prisoner of war for 16 months. He found a volleyball in his prisoner of war camp and spent hours working on his ball handling and passing. When he returned to school he used his skills to become the team's most effective dribbler and passer.

Neither Jones nor Beard got off to great starts in their Kentucky careers.

Beard scored only two points in his debut game (against Fort Knox) and it took Jones seven games before he broke into double figures.

CHAPTER 2

To Stay and Play or Go Away

The 1945-46 team was succeeding, with veteran stars -- juniors Jack Tingle and Jack Parkinson leading the way, but Beard was having trouble adjusting to Coach Rupp's caustic methods.

After one game in which he went scoreless for the first time in his life, Beard went home to Louisville to visit his mother.

He was so upset he broke down and cried.

"I just wish I was dead," he sobbed.

His mother cradled him in her arms and gently patted him on his back.

"Ralph you are still just a young boy. Those fellas you are playing with and against are all older than you. Just give yourself time to adjust. You know you are as good as anybody, anywhere," she told him. "Believe in yourself. I believe in you, and so do a lot of others. Play hard and everything will work out."

Beard had a talk with Tingle about his problems as they sat together shortly before Christmas of 1945, having a glass of milk at the school cafeteria.

"Jack, I don't think I can s-s-stand any more of Coach Rupp's constant sarcastic criticism. I never seem to do anything to p-p-please him," Beard said. "I'm thinking about leaving, going back home."

"C'mon, Ralph," said Tingle. "We need you out there. We got a chance to win the national championship with you."

"Well, podnah, I'm not so sure Coach Rupp feels that way. He is a-a-always on my ass about sump'n or another."

"He gets on all of us – you know that. He treats us all like shit – that's just the way he operates. But his bark is worse than his bite. He wants to win, of course, but he wants us to succeed individually as well," said Tingle, chugging down

15

the last of his milk. "Coach has always been arrogant, scathing, cantankerous, uncompromising, ruthless, vain, mean. He wants us all to hate him. But in the end he wants us all to succeed. That's just his way of getting us over the top. He once told one of our players 'I don't care if your girlfriend leaves you or your pet rabbit dies. I just care if you produce for me on the basketball court.'"

"I talked to my mom and told her I was seriously thinking about coming home, maybe p-p-playing at the University of Louisville," said Beard. "She said I was just young and homesick and I should really think t-t-twice about leaving."

"Your mom is right. We have a great bunch of guys here . . . not only talented guys, but good Joes. We really, really want you to stay, Ralph."

"Guess I will talk to Coach Rupp about things and see h-h-how that goes," said Beard. "I'll letchya know how it comes out."

That afternoon Beard was in Coach Rupp's office, sheepishly sitting across from him with his head down.

Rupp placed his elbows on his desk, cupped his chin in his hands and looked across at Beard for several seconds, waiting for Beard to speak.

Finally, Beard raised his head. "Coach, it seems that I am n-n-not doing so well for the team and I have been thinking about the idea of maybe l-l-leaving and going back home to Louisville, playing for U of L."

Rupp sat silent for a minute, then leaned back in his chair.

Then, in his native Kansas twang, said, "Young man, I have had many great basketball players come through this office. Quite a few of them in their freshman year get homesick. They were big stars in high school and were not used to coaches yelling at them and getting on their asses and telling them how much they were screwing up on the court. I guess you might say I am something of a perfectionist when it comes to basketball. But I am also a realist – I know no one can be perfect all the time. But, still, that should be your goal. And that means I may frequently call your attention to your imperfections so that you can move closer to your goal of perfection. Young man, I think you have great potential to be one of the best basketball players who have ever worn the Blue and White. But if you have set your mind on transferring to the Normal School, I won't stand in your way. And, by Gawd, we sure won't cancel the season because you're gone."

Beard sat somewhat stunned. It seemed obvious Coach Rupp was going to continue using his methods, no matter what Beard decided.

"Coach, maybe I just n-n-need some growing up, like my mom says. I'm still a teenager with half a brain, I reckon. I think I will just stick it out with our t-t-team and hope to make you happier before the season is over," said Beard.

Coach Rupp stood up and extended his hand. Smiling, he said, "You're a good boy, Ralph, I know everything will work out."

And things did work out, indeed.

Beard went on to score in double figures 12 games his freshman year, but his numbers would have been even better had he not had a poor 51.8 per cent shooting percentage from the free throw line. But he was a ball of fire as a playmaker and a fierce defensive demon. He led the team in steals and assists, though no official stats were kept in those categories.

Beard always drew the opposing team's best backcourt player as his defensive assignment. Prior to one game, Coach Rupp told Beard he was going to have to guard the other team's star guard. "I expect you to strangle him," Rupp said.

Beard was obsessed with trying to hold his man down defensively.

As he lay asleep in his dorm bed the night before the game, Beard startled some of his teammates when he suddenly sat up in bed with his hands wrapped around his pillow in a strangle hold yelling, "I gotcha now, Burl, you sumbitch, I gotcha now," said Beard.

"Wake up, Ralph, you're having a nightmare," said Tingle.

Wah Wah Jones also had a productive freshman season, scoring in double figures 17 times and leading the team in rebounding.

Kentucky in March 1946 won the prestigious NIT Tournament in New York City, beating Arizona 77-53, West Virginia 59-51 and Rhode Island 46-45.

They finished the season with a 28-2 record (losing a close game to Temple – later avenged – and a close game to Notre Dame). They were generally considered by some sports media organizations as the No. 1 team in the country.

The Wildcats did not play in the NCAA that season. At that time the NCAA was an invitational tournament, with teams selected by a committee. UK did not receive an invitation, greatly irritating Rupp, even though the NIT was considered as big – or bigger – a tournament at the time.

The NCAA tournament of 1946 had eight teams: Baylor, Harvard, NYU, North Carolina, Ohio State, Oklahoma A&M, California and Colorado. Oklahoma A&M beat North Carolina 43-40 in the championship game.

"That was one of the biggest mistakes the NCAA ever made, as far as I am concerned," said Rupp. "I felt we could have beaten any of those NCAA tournament teams."

The NIT tournament was March 16-20 and the NCAA tournament was March 21-26. So, it was possible for UK to have played in both, though the travel arrangements might have been tough.

Several UK players won all-star honors for 1945-46, including:

Junior Jack Parkinson (6-0), All-American; junior Jack Tingle (6-3), All-American; freshman Jones, All-SEC; freshman Beard, All-SEC, and senior Wilbur Schu (6-4), All-SEC (2nd Team).

UK player statistics for 1945-46

Player	Games Played	FG	FT	FTA	%	F	Total Pts	PPG
Jack Parkinson	30	143	53	76	69.7	44	339	11.3
Wallace Jones	30	105	80	126	63.5	83	290	9.67
Ralph Beard	30	111	57	110	51.8	69	279	9.3
Jack Tingle	30	117	44	64	68.8	68	278	9.27
Wilbur Schu	26	71	58	82	70.7	45	200	7.69
Joe Holland	30	60	20	35	57.1	42	140	4.67
Mulford Davis	13	14	12	22	54.5	18	40	3.08
Kenton Campbell	28	34	14	28	50	21	82	2.93
Darrell Lorance	11	10	9	10	90	12	29	2.64
J. Ed Parker	26	26	12	24	50	34	64	2.46
Malcolm McMullen	8	7	3	8	37.5	5	17	2.13
Sam Zeaman	1	1	0	0	0	1	2	2
William Sturgill	22	17	4	10	40	13	38	1.73
Deward Compton	6	4	2	4	50	2	10	1.67
Jim Weber	6	2	1	7	14.3	1	5	.83
Ed Allin	10	2	2	6	33.3	6	6	.6
Zeb Blankenship	6	1	0	0	0	5	2	.33
Johnny Crockett	1	0	0	0	0	1	0	0
Bob Hehl	1	0	0	0	0	0	0	0
Barkley Sturgill	1	0	0	0	0	0	0	0

Team results for UK's 28-2 season of 1945-46

Date	Game	Result	Score	Notes
12/1/1945	Ft. Knox at Kentucky	W	59 - 34	-
12/7/1945	Western Ontario at Kentucky	W	51 - 42	-
12/8/1945	Western Ontario at Kentucky	W	71 - 28	-
12/15/1945	Cincinnati at Kentucky	W	67 - 31	-
12/18/1945	Arkansas at Kentucky	W	67 - 42	-
12/21/1945	Oklahoma at Kentucky	W	43 - 33	-
12/29/1945	Kentucky vs. St. Johns	W	73 - 59	(at New York, NY)
1/1/1946	Kentucky at Temple	L	45 - 53	-
1/5/1946	Ohio at Kentucky	W	57 - 48	-
1/7/1946	Fort Benning at Kentucky	W	81 - 25	-
1/12/1946	Kentucky at Michigan State	W	55 - 44	-
1/14/1946	Kentucky at Xavier	W	62 - 36	-
1/19/1946	Kentucky at Tennessee	W	50 - 32	-
1/21/1946	Kentucky at Georgia Tech	W	68 - 43	-

Date	Matchup	Result	Score	Notes
1/26/1946	Kentucky vs. Notre Dame	L	47 - 56	(at Louisville, KY)
1/28/1946	Georgia Tech at Kentucky	W	54 - 26	-
2/2/1946	Michigan State at Kentucky	W	59 - 51	-
2/4/1946	Kentucky at Vanderbilt	W	59 - 37	-
2/9/1946	Kentucky vs. Vanderbilt	W	64 - 31	(at Paducah, KY)
2/16/1946	Tennessee at Kentucky	W	54 - 34	-
2/19/1946	Kentucky at Ohio	W	60 - 52	-
2/23/1946	Xavier at Kentucky	W	83 - 40	-
2/28/1946	Kentucky vs. Auburn	W	69 - 24	SEC Tournament (at Louisville, KY)
3/1/1946	Kentucky vs. Florida	W	69 - 32	SEC Tournament (at Louisville, KY)
3/2/1946	Kentucky vs. Alabama	W	59 - 30	SEC Tournament (at Louisville, KY)
3/2/1946	Kentucky vs. Louisiana State	W	59 - 36	SEC Tournament Championship (at Louisville, KY)
3/9/1946	Kentucky vs. Temple	W	54 - 43	(at Louisville, KY)
3/16/1946	Kentucky vs. Arizona	W	77 - 53	NIT (at New York, NY)
3/18/1946	Kentucky vs. West Virginia	W	59 - 51	NIT (at New York, NY)
3/20/1946	Kentucky vs. Rhode Island	W	46 - 45	NIT Championship (at New York, NY)

The 1946-47 season prospects looked great, with so many stars returning and with Alex Groza coming back after serving a stint in the Army.

Groza as a skinny 6-5 freshman had led the 1944-45 team in the first half of the season, averaging more than 16 points a game through his first 10 games. But it was at that point in January he was drafted into the Army and would not return until the 1946-47 season.

When Groza got drafted a reporter asked Coach Rupp why he was so upset to see that happen. "Well, we are going to miss that young man very much," said the coach.

The reporter asked Rupp why Groza was so important inasmuch as there was a lot of other talent on the UK team.

"But you don't replace a Caruso with a barbershop singer," Rupp replied.

While in the Army, Groza worked in a military hospital, but spent most of his time playing for military basketball teams. He earned all-service honors with the Fort Hood, Texas, team.

Rupp was delighted when Groza returned for 1946-47, two inches taller and 70 pounds heavier (220).

In the fall of 1946 Groza and Beard became friends as the team prepared for the season.

Groza came to UK from Martins Ferry, Ohio, High School, where he twice made all-state and scored a state-record 628 points as a senior in 1944. He was honorary captain of the All-Ohio high school team and had hoped to play for Ohio State University, where his brother, 6-3 Lou Groza, was a star football player destined to become an NFL great as a kicker and offensive tackle.

But, strangely, OSU wasn't interested, and UK was the only big school to offer him a scholarship.

CHAPTER 2

Basketball or Football . . .or Both

Beard and Groza sat in their athletic dorm in October 1946 talking about their chances of capturing a national championship in 1946-47.

"Looking at our schedule, I don't t-t-think we will have any trouble in the SEC, though Tennessee and Alabama will probably be d-d-decent," said Beard, lying on his bunk and leafing through a magazine.

"Yeah, I agree," said Groza. "But we have Temple and Notre Dame on our schedule, too. They could be tough."

Groza walked over and grabbed ahold of Beard's shoulders. Beard had separated both shoulders playing football as a freshman, one of the reasons he got off to a slow start in basketball that fall.

"Your shoulders gonna be okay for basketball this season, Ralph?" said Groza.

"Yeah, Beak (the nickname teammates had given Groza because of his prominent nose), but I t-t-told Coach Bryant (Bear Bryant, who became the UK coach in 1946) that I was going to give up f-f-football and concentrate on basketball."

"Good idea – glad to hear it," said Groza. "I wish Wah (Wah Wah Jones) would do the same thing. I worry all the time about him possibly getting hurt. He means a lot to our basketball team."

"Yeah, me, too. But Wah made all-SEC as a tight end and it will be h-h-hard for him to give up football," said Beard.

Coach Bryant and Coach Rupp had quickly become very good friends and each was a big supporter of both football and basketball.

They had a meeting in Rupp's office in late October 1946 after Bryant had led UK to a 7-3 record in his first season after the team had lost 8 of 10 in 1945.

Coach Bryant was carrying a sheaf of papers and dropped them on Coach Rupp's desk.

"Adolph, this is the statistics for each of our games this season. As you can see, Wah Wah Jones was one of our most important players. Now, I hear that you have suggested to him that he drop football from here on and concentrate on just basketball. Is that true?" said Coach Bryant.

Coach Rupp leaned back in his chair and crossed his arms across his chest. There was a hint of a wry smile on his face.

"Now, Bear, where did you hear such a thing?"

"A couple of my players told me Wah Wah was saying he was considering playing basketball only because he felt that was what you wanted," said Coach Bryant, taking a seat.

"The only thing I told Wah was that I thought his best chance to become a professional athlete was in the sport of basketball," said Coach Rupp. "I never exactly told him he should give up football. But I think you will agree with me that Wah's future is in basketball, not football."

"Not necessarily," said Coach Bryant, picking up the sheaf of papers, which Coach Rupp had ignored. "He's good enough to be a pro football prospect. Frankly, he's the best tight end I have ever seen, college or pro. He could block out a Mack coal truck if I asked him to. He has tackled the quarterback more than any defensive end I have ever coached. And, he is a great pass-catcher, too. He is great on both sides of the ball."

"Well, coach, I can appreciate your dilemma," said Coach Rupp. "You inherited a bad situation with Kentucky football. I think you are the man who can get this football program back on its feet and I want to do everything I can to support you. But basketball is Number 1 at Kentucky and I want it to continue that way. If you can bring UK football up to the point where UK basketball is right now, then I will be the first person in line to shake your hand. But I personally don't think any man could ever do that. Basketball will always be king."

"Well, coach, I think I will prove you are wrong about that," said Coach Bryant, reaching across and shaking Coach Rupp's hand. "We may not do it overnight, but I think we will reach your level within a few years, but I need players like Wah to help us get there."

"Fine, fine," said Coach Rupp. "I have a great love for this university and I want it to be successful in all fields -- sports and academics. I have had very few players who could ever manage to be successful in both football and basketball, and I believe Wah is one of the rare exceptions to that. I hate it that he is out there endangering his basketball career. But, I am not going to do anything to discourage Wah from playing football for you. I just pray he doesn't get hurt out there and lose his chance for a professional basketball career."

Coach Bryant smiled broadly. "Coach, I appreciate your candor and honesty. Let's both keep our fingers crossed that this young man helps elevate both our programs."

Jones had several teeth knocked loose and suffered numerous cuts and bruises and ankle injuries while playing football in the 1940s era in which players had no helmet face masks and relatively little uniform padding, but he never suffered a serious enough football injury to keep him out of any significant basketball action, including an emergency appendectomy. But he was slowed considerably at the start of his sophomore season, scoring only 40 points in his first 14 games.

In one football game Wah Wah had several teeth knocked loose and returned to the sideline spitting out a mouthful of blood.

Coach Bryant put his hand on Wah's shoulder and ordered him back into the game. Wah Wah showed him his bloody mouth and Coach Bryant said, "Get back in there . . . you don't run on your teeth."

Wah Wah had managed to escape the draft in high school because when he was called to visit the draft board he showed up with a gimpy foot and was excused from duty.

Humzey Yessin, a UK basketball team manager, became friends with Jones and told everyone that Jones getting a military exemption did not go over well with the opponents of the Harlan Green Devils.

"All the Kentucky high schools, every time there was a draft called, everybody wanted him on that bus. They all said if he could shoot a basketball that well, he should be able to shoulder a rifle."

"He was the last UK four-sport man," Yessin said. In addition to basketball and football, Jones was a pitcher with the Wildcats and a member of the UK track and field squad.

"You didn't want to press him too much or you were going to wind up on your backside," Joe B. Hall, who was a onetime teammate of Jones at UK and later became the head coach, succeeding the retired Rupp.

"Rupp used to call him 'the killer,'" Yessin said. "Wah could really block his man out and get the rebound, then get the ball out on a fast break."

Yessin said because of Jones, the offense was pretty simple.

"We ran a two-guard offense and the forward was the key in there. Wah could block his man and hand it off to Beard," Yessin said. "It was old number six. Rupp used to say, 'Well, first there is the National Anthem and then we run No. 6.' That was the offense."

At the University of Kentucky, Jones was a member of the Phi Delta Theta Fraternity.

The Wildcats finished 1946-47 with a regular season record of 32-2, losing only to Oklahoma A&M 31-27 in the Sugar Bowl tournament title game and to DePaul 43-37 in Chicago.

"Our boys were just too damn overconfident in that Sugar Bowl game against A&M," said Rupp. "They just sleep walked through that one."

Astonishingly, the Wildcats again were shunned by the NCAA.

Kentucky went on to play in the prestigious NIT in New York City, beating Long Island 66-62 and North Carolina State 60-42 before losing 49-45 to Utah in the championship game to finish the season at 34-3.

The NCAA field of 1947 included Navy, Holy Cross, CCNY, Wisconsin, Oklahoma, Texas and Wyoming and Oregon State. Holy Cross beat Oklahoma 58-47 for the title.

But the Wildcats were never again going to be denied NCAA tournament invitations.

Individual statistics for the UK 34-3 season of 1946-47:

Player	Games Played	FG	FGA	%	FT	FTA	%	F	Total Pts	PPG
Alex Groza	37	146	372	39.2	101	160	63.1	85	393	10.62
Ralph Beard	37	157	469	33.5	78	115	67.8	71	392	10.59
Ken Rollins	37	112	365	30.7	86	107	80.4	81	310	8.38
Wallace Jones	33	87	302	28.8	43	78	55.1	38	217	6.58
Joe Holland	37	96	337	28.5	32	58	55.2	70	224	6.05
Jim Line	35	86	209	41.1	27	40	67.5	47	199	5.69
Jack Tingle	37	90	355	25.4	22	40	55	71	202	5.46
Bob Brannum	29	49	158	31	27	51	52.9	68	125	4.31
Cliff Barker	34	52	161	32.3	16	31	51.6	27	120	3.53

Mulford Davis	16	24	62	38.7	6	10	60	14	54	3.38
James Jordan	28	31	131	23.7	18	27	66.7	31	80	2.86
J. Ed Parker	35	33	100	33	28	39	71.8	36	94	2.69
Dale Barnstable	27	32	96	33.3	7	9	77.8	15	71	2.63
Kenton Campbell	15	10	-	?	2	-	?	6	22	1.47
Albert Cummins	21	9	32	28.1	2	3	66.7	7	20	.95
Malcolm McMullen	13	2	14	14.3	3	7	42.9	11	7	.54

UK's schedule results for 1946-47

Date	Game	Result	Score	Notes
11/28/1946	Indiana Central at Kentucky	W	78 - 36	-
11/30/1946	Tulane at Kentucky	W	64 - 35	-
12/2/1946	Ft. Knox at Kentucky	W	68 - 31	-
12/7/1946	Kentucky at Cincinnati	W	80 - 49	-
12/9/1946	Idaho at Kentucky	W	65 - 35	-
12/12/1946	Kentucky vs. DePaul	W	65 - 45	(at Louisville, KY)
12/14/1946	Texas A & M at Kentucky	W	83 - 18	-
12/16/1946	Miami (OH) at Kentucky	W	62 - 49	-
12/21/1946	Kentucky vs. St. Johns	W	70 - 50	(at New York, NY)
12/23/1946	Baylor at Kentucky	W	75 - 34	-
12/28/1946	Wabash at Kentucky	W	96 - 24	-
12/30/1946	Kentucky vs. Oklahoma A&M	L	31 - 37	Sugar Bowl (at New Orleans, LA)
1/4/1947	Ohio at Kentucky	W	46 - 36	-
1/11/1947	Dayton at Kentucky	W	70 - 29	-
1/13/1947	Kentucky at Vanderbilt	W	82 - 30	-
1/18/1947	Kentucky at Tennessee	W	54 - 39	-

Date	Opponent	Result	Score	Notes
1/20/1947	Kentucky at Georgia Tech	W	70 - 47	-
1/21/1947	Kentucky at Georgia	W	84 - 45	-
1/25/1947	Xavier at Kentucky	W	71 - 34	-
1/27/1947	Michigan State at Kentucky	W	86 - 36	-
2/1/1947	Kentucky vs. Notre Dame	W	60 - 30	(at Louisville, KY)
2/3/1947	Kentucky at Alabama	W	48 - 37	-
2/8/1947	Kentucky at DePaul	L	47 - 53	-
2/10/1947	Georgia at Kentucky	W	81 - 40	
2/15/1947	Tennessee at Kentucky	W	61 - 46	-
2/17/1947	Alabama at Kentucky	W	63 - 33	-
2/19/1947	Kentucky at Xavier	W	58 - 31	-
2/21/1947	Vanderbilt at Kentucky	W	84 - 41	-
2/22/1947	Georgia Tech at Kentucky	W	83 - 46	-
2/27/1947	Kentucky vs. Vanderbilt	W	98 - 29	SEC Tournament (at Louisville, KY)
2/28/1947	Kentucky vs. Auburn	W	84 - 18	SEC Tournament (at Louisville, KY)
3/1/1947	Kentucky vs. Georgia Tech	W	75 - 53	SEC Tournament (at Louisville, KY)
3/1/1947	Kentucky vs. Tulane	W	55 - 38	SEC Tournament Championship (at Louisville, KY)
3/8/1947	Kentucky vs. Temple	W	68 - 29	(at Louisville, KY)
3/17/1947	Kentucky vs. Long	W	66 -	NIT (at New York, NY)

	Island		62	
3/19/1947	Kentucky vs. N. C. State	W	60 - 42	NIT (at New York, NY)
3/24/1947	Kentucky vs. Utah	L	45 - 49	NIT Championship (at New York, NY)

After the 1945-46 season Wah Wah's little brother, Hugh Jones Jr., was finishing his career at Harlan High. He was an outstanding player, just like his big brother.

Wah Wah had hoped Hugh would join him at UK for the 1946-47 season, but Rupp had too much talent to add him to the team.

Coach Rupp talked to Wah Wah about the idea of letting his little brother join the Wildcats.

"Now, Wah Wah your little brother is an excellent player, but he just would not fit in here at UK with the players we now have," Rupp told Wah Wah. "He just needs to go to Tennessee or someplace like that where he can get some good playing time."

Hugh Jones wound up signing with Tennessee. UK won 10 of the 11 games he played against the Wildcats. Hugh scored 74 points in the 11 games, including 9 in Tennessee's 66-53 win over UK on Jan. 14, 1950, and had his career high against UK when he got 13 in a 95-58 loss to UK on March 4, 1950 in the SEC tournament.

Hugh went on to become two-time all-SEC second team (regular season and in the tournament).

Kentucky's incredible basketball success continued to grow. Under Rupp, the team developed a fast-break offense and pressing defense that was ahead of its time in an era in which most teams played a plodding style.

The Wildcats won NCAA championships in both 1947-48 and 1948-49, with Beard, Jones and Groza leading the way.

The Wildcats of 1947-48 earned the nickname "The Fabulous Five," with Beard, Groza, Jones, Kenny Rollins and Cliff Barker becoming legends in their own time. All but Rollins returned for the 1948-49 season.

The Fabulous Five 1948
Seated: Ralph Beard, Adolph Rupp, Kenny Rollins
Standing: Wallace "Wah Wah" Jones, Alex Groza, Cliff Barker

The UK players then added an Olympic title to their resume as their starting five became the core of the U. S. team that took home the gold medal in London in 1948.

Kentucky had become the nation's most successful college basketball program and had established a national dominance.

In that era the NCAA tournament only had Eastern and Western regions, with the regional winners playing for the national title each year.

Kentucky had a tough game against Holy Cross in the 1948 Eastern Regional finals. Holy Cross, led by basketball legend Bob Cousy, had won the 1947 NCAA title and many experts picked them to win again in 1948.

Here's how the UK-Holy Cross game went, according to a New York Time story by Louis Effrat:

NEW YORK, March 20, 1948 -- A Kentucky quintet that never stopped driving until the final two minutes, when victory was clinched, rode over scrappy Holy Cross, 60-52, and into the N.C.A.A. championship round last night at Madison Square Garden.

Wholly merited and earned, the triumph gave Adolph Rupp's Wildcats first place in the Eastern regional competition and qualified the Kentuckians for Tuesday night's final at the Garden against Baylor, the Western regional survivor. The Bears upset Kansas State, 60-52, at Kansas City last night.

Top-notch basketball was displayed by both sides at the Garden last night, but the Wildcats had the speed, the size and the shots. More important, they knew how to utilize these assets and, at one stage in the second half, enjoyed a 14-point margin. That the Crusaders from Worcester, Mass., fought back into contention later, cutting the deficit to four points, was indicative of their ability and determination.

In the end, however, Kentucky had what it needed to protect its advantage -- stamina. Two minutes before time ran out, the Wildcats were ahead, 57-50. The Crusaders, pressing all over the court, attempted to knock the leaders off stride, but they succeeded only in committing a half dozen fouls, all of which were waived. Poise, so vital in basketball, never deserted the Wildcats.

The 18,472 fans on hand saw more than an ordinary court struggle. Students of the game were thrilled by the individual duels that were going on, as the rival coaches, Rupp and Alvin (Doggy) Julian, master-minded every minute. Rupp's strategy prevailed because Ken Rollins and Dale Barnstable turned in magnificent jobs of defending against the brilliant Bob Cousy.

Then there was the individual battle between Kentucky's Alex Groza and Holy Cross' George Kaftan. There, again, the Wildcats finished on top, Groza outplaying Kaftan by a wide margin and tallying 23 points to annex the game's scoring laurels. And while all this was going on, Ralph Beard and Wallace (Wah Wah) Jones were running the Crusaders dizzy.

Because the Holy Cross players, vainly trying to add to a 19-game winning streak and protect an unbeaten record on the Eighth Avenue hardwood, were unable to stop Groza, Jones and Beard, it was inevitable that victory go to Kentucky. On the other hand, once it became apparent that the Wildcats had the formula to minimize the effectiveness of Cousy and Kaftan, the decision belonged, more or less, to Kentucky.

Cousy, limited to one field goal, wound up with five points, practically a shut-out for the prolific scorer whose outstanding work throughout the year sparked the Crusaders to one of their greatest records -- 25 wins and 3 losses -- up to last night. Cousy, who scored 472 points prior to this engagement, seldom was allowed room to get off his shots and much credit for a fine guarding chore must go to Rollins.

Kentucky, a 5-point favorite, lived up to its billing. From the outset, Rupp had his charges running at top speed and making the most of a fast break. But Holy Cross, with Kaftan doing a nice job, capitalized on slick ball-handling and, after three and a half minutes of the most spirited play witnessed all season, it was a 7-7 standstill.

Then the Wildcats, with Beard contributing handsomely, clicked for 5 straight points for a 12-7 lead and a headstart toward conquest. Never again did the Crusaders pull into a tie. At the half the count favored Kentucky, 36-28, and there was every indication that it might go higher.

However, following the rest period, the Crusaders came out full of fight, drove in for two quick baskets and suddenly it was a real contest again. Four points to the good, Kentucky called for a time-out. The Wildcats must have realized that Holy Cross, counting the closing minutes of the opening period, had amassed nine consecutive points.

That cessation did it. When play was resumed, the Wildcats hit for seven in a row. Jones succeeded with a one-hander, followed with a 2-pointer from the keyhole and, after a one-hander by Groza, Jones tossed in a foul shot. The Crusaders could not retrieve those points, and though they continued to battle, it was in a losing cause.

Groza's tap-ins were spectacular and the maneuvers of Beard won the fancy of the crowd, but if one were asked to point to the strongest feature of Kentucky's play, it would have to be its relentless driving. The Wildcats did a lot of digging and never tired. It was the inability of Holy Cross to cope with this power that led to defeat.

One thing is certain -- the East will have the strongest representation possible in Tuesday night's final. That's a fair-to-middlin' outfit that Rupp has assembled, an outfit which now has gained a berth in the Olympic playoffs.

The Cats went on to face Baylor in the finals. The game as reported in the Times:

Kentucky Defeats Baylor in N.C.A.A. Final at Garden

NEW YORK, March 23, 1948 -- Kentucky's Wildcats, at no time in jeopardy, easily conquered Baylor, 58-42, last night at Madison Square Garden and romped to their first N.C.A.A. basketball championship. Off to an early 17-point lead, Adolph Rupp's powerhouse completely outclassed the Bears from Waco, Texas.

The second smaller turnout of the season, 16,174, witnessed this one-sided East-West final, in which Baylor's strategy -- slowdown and stress possessions -- succeeded only in holding down the score. Baylor, lightly regarded at the outset of the Western Regionals, qualified for the title clash with a pair of upset victories over Washington and Kansas State, but last night ran out of surprises.

Perhaps the best way to describe Kentucky's thirty-fourth and certainly most important triumph of the campaign is to report that form held up. Nearly every pre-game prediction pointed to the size, speed and depth of the Wildcats from Lexington and figured that these would determine the outcome. They did, too, even if Coach Rupp, who wanted to win this one above all others, saw little need to turn to his bench. He did not substitute until 6:30 of the second half, by which time the decision was just about clinched.

Alex Groza, the tallest man on the floor, was the high scorer for Kentucky and the game. His 14 points were two more than Ralph Beard tallied and four more than Bill Johnson made for Baylor. The latter was unable to handle Groza's height and most of the rebounds were dominated by the 6-foot 7-inch center who was voted the outstanding player of the tournament.

But Groza was far from being the only Wildcat in a starring role. Beard, an irrepressible digger; Ken Rollins, an all-around ace; Wallace (Wah Wah) Jones, a dependable workhorse, along with the steady Cliff Barker -- all contributed handsomely toward a victorious cause.

That Baylor, because of Kentucky's height advantage, would resort to a deliberate style of attack, was anticipated. The Bears, reluctant to risk forfeiting possession, attempted to make certain that ever shot be a clear one and from close range. As a result they had taken only one chance in the first four minutes and six in the first seven and a half, not one finding the target.

Thus Kentucky enjoyed a 13-1 spread -- Jim Owen caged a foul shot at 5:25 -- and Baylor followers foresaw a rout.

Finally, when the clock showed 7 minutes and 35 seconds gone, Don Heathington dribbled in with a lay-up and the Texans, on their seventh attempt from the floor, achieved their initial basket.

However, this was not repeated often enough to lighten Baylor's burden and at 12:35 Kentucky's lead was 17 points at 24-7. This shrunk slightly to 29-15 at the intermission and later the Bears rallied to cut the deficit to 9 points, but the Wildcats packed too many weapons and triumphed going away.

Kentucky, obviously superior in all departments, was most impressive during the early stages. One 2-minute spurt netted 7 points as Jones, Rollins and Groza excelled.

The Wildcats were driving hard and harassing the Bears at every turn. Thereafter they performed commendably enough, but their rallies were intermittent and the Kentuckians did not again look that superb.

Probably the reason for this letup was lack of incentive. They were en route to victory and knew it, and no end of grimaces from Rupp on the bench sufficed to reawaken them. Baylor, on the other hand, did not have the power to take full advantage and suffered its sixth setback of the year.

In victory, Kentucky attempted a total of 83 shots, clicking with 23, as compared to 15 out of 64 for the losers. Both teams automatically qualified for the Olympic trials which get underway Saturday afternoon at the Garden.

Third place in the competition went to Holy Cross, despite an early 16-point lead, staggering to a 60-54 victory over Kansas State in the preliminary encounter.

Kentucky 58

Player	FG	FT	FTA	PF	Pts
Wallace Jones	4	1	1	3	9
Cliff Barker	2	1	3	4	5
Jim Line	3	1	1	3	7
Alex Groza	6	2	4	4	14
Joe Holland	1	0	0	1	2
Ralph Beard	4	4	4	1	12
Ken Rollins	3	3	5	3	9
Dale Barnstable	0	0	1	0	0
Totals	23	12	19	19	58

Baylor 42 *(Head Coach: Bill Henderson)*

Player	FG	FT	FTA	PF	Pts
James 'Red' Owen	2	1	2	0	5
Bill DeWitt	3	2	4	3	8
Bill Hickman	1	0	0	0	2
Ralph Pulley	0	1	1	0	1
Don Heathington	3	2	4	5	8
Odell Preston	0	0	2	2	0
Bill Johnson	3	4	7	5	10
Jack Robinson	3	2	4	4	8
Bill Srack	0	0	0	0	0
Totals	15	12	24	19	42

UK player statistics for 1947-48

Player	Games Played	FG	FGA	%	FT	FTA	%	F	Total Pts	PPG
Ralph Beard	38	194	536	36.2	88	149	59.1	80	476	12.53
Alex Groza	39	200	530	37.7	88	140	62.9	87	488	12.51
Wallace Jones	36	133	427	31.1	69	103	67	82	335	9.31
Jim Line	38	107	296	36.1	51	62	82.3	72	265	6.97
Ken Rollins	39	95	341	27.9	67	92	72.8	90	257	6.59
Cliff Barker	38	98	317	30.9	52	93	55.9	101	248	6.53
Dale Barnstable	38	76	280	27.1	24	42	57.1	55	176	4.63
Joe Holland	38	58	207	28	24	47	51.1	69	140	3.68
Jack Parkinson	29	43	214	20.1	10	22	45.5	33	96	3.31
Walter Hirsch	13	16	55	29.1	5	9	55.6	8	37	2.85
Albert Cummins	17	13	37	35.1	6	9	66.7	13	32	1.88
Roger Day	11	5	18	27.8	7	9	77.8	8	17	1.55
Mike Homa	2	1	-		1	1	100	3	3	1.5
James Jordan	30	13	88	14.8	18	25	72	19	44	1.47
Garland Townes	13	7	22	31.8	5	11	45.5	6	19	1.46
Will Smethers	7	5	10	50	0	3	0	4	10	1.43
Robert Henne	11	5	22	22.7	3	7	42.9	7	13	1.18
Kenton Campbell	15	6	27	22.2	4	7	57.1	10	16	1.07
John Stough	23	8	38	21.1	5	10	50	20	21	.91

The NCAA championship did not end Kentucky's season in 1948.

Since 1948 was an Olympics year (the Olympics were resumed after a 12-year hiatus due to the war), the U. S. had to put together its official hoops team to represent the country in the Summer Games in London.

The Olympics committee decided to conduct Olympics trials involving college teams, and the semi-pro AAU teams, such as the Phillips Oilers (a team composed of former college stars).

First up was a matchup pitting Kentucky against arch rival Louisville.

The Cardinals had won a qualifying tournament in Kansas City and got their shot at the top-ranked Wildcats in New York City.

Rupp met with his team at their New York hotel to discuss the upcoming game against the Cardinals.

"Boys, I am sure Louisville has a nice team and we will have to work hard to get a win," said Rupp. "But I am here to tell you I am sick and tired of all the yammering I am hearing from

Cardinal fans. They have been banging on my hotel door, hollering at me everywhere I go. They keep telling me their boys are going to kick our butts and show everyone who the real national champions are. Now, I hope you go out there and prove that you are the national champions, no doubt about it."

Kentucky left no doubt, beating the Cardinals 91-57 in their first Olympics trials test.

Kentucky 91

Player	FG	FT	FTA	PF	Pts
Cliff Barker	4	5	8	4	13
Wallace Jones	7	5	7	2	19
Jim Line	4	0	1	2	8
John Stough	0	0	0	1	0
Alex Groza	5	2	4	3	12
Joe Holland	2	1	1	3	5
Ken Rollins	2	0	0	5	4
Dale Barnstable	3	0	0	2	6
Ralph Beard	10	2	4	3	22
James Jordan	0	2	3	1	2
Totals	37	17	28	26	91

Louisville 57 *(Head Coach: Peck Hickman)*

Player	FG	FT	FTA	PF	Pts
Jack Coleman	4	2	3	5	10
Glenn Combs	3	4	4	3	10
Bob Borah	0	3	4	3	3
Jim Edwards	0	0	0	0	0
Deward Compton (*)	3	3	3	4	9
Oz Johnson	1	1	2	4	3
Kenny Reeves	1	3	5	0	5
Johnny Knopf	3	1	3	3	7
Roy Combs	3	4	5	0	10
Paul Walker	0	0	0	0	0
Totals	18	21	29	22	57

Kentucky then faced a rematch with Bayor and won that one easily 77-59.

The Cats were then pitted against the Phillips Oilers in an exhibition match in New York and lost 53-49.

"Our boys were real tired for that game," said Rupp. We had played nine tournament games in two weeks and the boys' legs were just about gone. Phillips had hardly played at all, so they were well rested."

The Wildcats went up against the Oilers three more exhibition games in July 1948 winning one and losing two. There was no significant professional basketball league at the time and the best former college players joined company-sponsored AAU teams, such as the Oilers (sponsored by Phillips Oil Co.). They were, in effect, professionals. In 1937, the **National Basketball League**, often abbreviated to **NBL**, was a professional men's basketball league with a limited number of teams and was basically inferior to the AAU at the time. The league later merged with the Basketball Association of America (BAA) to form the National Basketball Association (NBA) in 1949.

Phillips Oilers were led by 7-0 Bob Kurland, who was the star of the Oklahoma A&M teams which won NCAA championships in 1945-46.

Kurland was famous for leaping up and batting away or grabbing opponent's shots before they went into the basket. He normally just hung around the basket, like a vulture.

At that time the free throw lane was only six feet wide. The lane was not widened until 1951. The three-second rule had been enacted in 1936 but the narrow lane still allowed big centers to linger close to the basket.

It was primarily because of Kurland's ability to sweep shots off the rim the NCAA instituted the goaltending rule the next season and the rule is still in use.

But the rule was not in effect during the Kentucky/Oilers series and it was primarily the goaltending work by Kurland that cost the Cats three close losses.

"That young man had already gone through college and he was much older and more mature than my boys," said Rupp. "He was seven feet tall, a giant for the game at that time, and he just stayed around under the basket and grabbed a lot of my boy's shots right before they went in. It was a huge advantage for the Oilers and was really unfair. They finally outlawed such stuff, but it was too late for us at that time. Thankfully, those games were just exhibitions and never counted on our record."

The NCAA selection committee finally decided five Kentucky players and five players from the Phillips Oilers would constitute the basic U. S. Olympic team, with Rupp as one of the coaches. Four more at-large players were added to the team. The final team roster included Bob Kurland, Gordon Carpenter, Clifford Barker, Don Barksdale, Ralph Beard, Lewis Beck, Vincent Boryla, Alex Groza, Wah Wah Jones, Ray Lumpp, Robert Pitts, Jesse Renick, Jack Robinson, Ken Rollins. By virtue of winning the UK/Oilers series the Phillips coach, Omar Browning, was named the head coach, to be assisted by Adolph Rupp.

But the Wildcats players proved to be the core of the squad.

The Kentucky-led team won their Olympic opener over Switzerland 86-21 and the game was described this way by Ted Smits of the AP in the Lexington Leader:

U.S. Romps 86-21 In Cage Opener; Groza Bags 19

WEMBLEY, England, July 30 - Uncle Sam's basketball forces led off with an easy victory as expected today as competition in six sports began in the Olympic games.

Coach Bud Browning's rangy, sharpshooting cagers conquered Switzerland 86-21 in the first round of the preliminaries.

With seven-foot Bob Kurland playing only part of the game because of fouling out, a University of Kentucky sharpshooter, Alex Groza, led the scoring for the United States forces, ringing in 19 points.

Browning was not fully satisfied with the Americans' performance. He said his boys were confused by the officials because their signals "are different than ours."

Midway of the game he ordered his team to quit faking shots. He said the Swiss reactions were so slow they weren't falling for the maneuvers.

U. S. 86

Player	FG	FT	FTA	PF	Pts
Lewis Beck	0	1	2	1	1
Wallace Jones	4	0	2	1	8
Ralph Beard	3	0	1	0	6
Ray Lumpp	4	0	0	4	8
Bob Kurland	4	1	2	4	9
Alex Groza	9	1	2	3	19
Cliff Barker	2	1	2	3	5
Jesse Renick	7	0	1	0	14
R.C. Pitts	6	0	0	1	12
Robert Robinson	2	0	1	1	4
Totals	41	4	13	18	86

Switzerland 21

Player	FG	FT	FTA	PF	Pts
Marc Bossy	1	0	2	4	2
Jean Pollett	0	1	3	3	1
Georges Stockly	1	1	3	4	3
Robert Geiser	0	0	1	1	0
Pierre Albrecht	2	1	2	0	5
Henri Baumann	0	1	3	0	1
Claude Chevalley	1	1	5	1	3
Bernard Dutoit	1	0	0	0	2
Hans Gujer	0	1	1	0	1
Claude Landini	1	1	1	0	3
Totals	7	7	21	13	21

In their second Olympics game the United States beat Czechoslovakia 53-28. The game write-up in the Lexington Leader:

U.S. Cagers Swamp Czechoslovakia, 53 to 28

European Champs Are No Match for Yankee Team

LONDON, Aug. 2 (AP) -- America's wizards of the court punctured any doubts of their Olympic basketball invincibility today by scoring a leisurely 53 - to - 28 triumph over Czechoslovakia, the best team in all Europe.

The Americans' mastery was so complete that the Phillips Oilers' seven-foot Bob Kurland, who can dunk the ball in the basket with the mildest sort of a leap, never once indulged in this advantage.

He took aim only when a sorting distance out on the floor and he cashed in a couple of these which, with two free throws, gave him six points for the day.

Vince Boryla of the Denver Nuggets led the point-making with nine -- four fielders and a free toss -- as Uncle Sam's nephews scattered the honors among nine of the 10 players to see action.

Only Alex Groza, of the University of Kentucky's brilliant shot maker, failed to register a point and he was removed from the contest early on personal fouls.

Gordon Carpenter and Louis Beck of the Phillips Oilers, and Ralph Beard of the University of Kentucky, racked up seven points apiece to follow Boryla in the scoring department.

U.S. Coach Omar (Bud) Browning mixed up his players. Never once did he send in a full five man squad of the Phillips Oilers, the great National Champion AAU team from Bartlesville, Okla. or the University of Kentucky Wildcats, who dominated U.S. college ranks last season.

A segment of the crowd of 1,250 hooted and laughed as Kurland and his towering teammates toyed with their adversaries.

The Americans led 23-12 at half time. The Czechs used a tight defense and their alert ball-handling made a good show of it.

This was the second victory for the Americans in Group C - one of the four divisions of round-robin eliminations.

The two top teams of each division qualify for places in the eight-team tournament proper.

U. S. 53

Player	FG	FT	FTA	PF	Pts
Lewis Beck	3	1	2	0	7
Jesse Renick	1	0	0	2	2
Ralph Beard	2	3	5	3	7
Cliff Barker	2	1	2	2	5
Don Barksdale	1	2	3	3	4
Bob Kurland	2	2	2	3	6
Vince Boryla	4	1	2	2	9
Gordon Carpenter	3	1	3	1	7
Ken Rollins	3	0	0	1	6
Alex Groza	0	0	1	4	0
Totals	**21**	**11**	**20**	**21**	**53**

Czechoslovakia 28

Player	FG	FT	FTA	PF	Pts
Jiri Siegel	1	0	0	4	2
Ivan Mrazek	3	2	4	2	8
Jan Kozak	0	3	5	0	3
Josef Krepela	2	3	6	2	7
Joseph Belohradsky	0	0	1	1	0
Cyril Benacek	1	5	5	1	7
Ladislav Trpkos	0	1	3	4	1
Jiri Drvota	0	0	1	1	0
Josef Ezr	0	0	0	0	0
Vaclav Krasa	0	0	0	2	0
Totals	**7**	**14**	**25**	**17**	**28**

In their third game the U. S. had their toughest outing of the tournament, reported this way by the New York Times:

American Rally Beats Argentina In Olympic Basketball, 59 to 57

Losers in Front at Half in Rough Contest, 33-26 - Lead Changes Hands Six Times - Kurland and Beard Inactive

LONDON, Aug. 3 (AP) - The United States basketball team that had been supposed to find the Olympics a breeze ran into a cyclone instead today and barely escaped with a 59-57 victory over Argentina.

Behind, 33-26, at the half and completely bewildered by the Argentines' surprising show of strength, the Americans simply bulled their way out of the jam.

The second half was rough, with guarding so tight, bodies constantly were banging into each other. Twice activities were interrupted by arguments over official rulings.

The Americans registered both protests. They complained the Argentines crowded them too closely under the goal during free throws. They also objected to the South Americans' final goal.

This was a looping shot taken by Ricardo Gonzalez, guard, just as the final gun sounded. The United States players contended it had been thrown too late. The officials held that it should count.

Six times the lead changed hands in the hard-driving battle and the United States did not go to the front to stay until only three minutes remained. A goal by the University of Kentucky's Alex Groza put the Americans ahead, 55-53, and they held the advantage despite the Argentines' rugged onslaughts.

America's galaxy of individual stars was dimmed by a rangy Argentine center named Oscar Furlong. Furlong not only spearheaded the South Americans' flashy floor game but scored 18 points to lead all single performances. He cashed in ten of his eleven tries form the free-throw lane.

United States Coach Omar (Bud) Browning called Furlong "one of the finest ball players I ever saw."

"He's like Jack McCracken (former Amateur Athletic Union star) in his heyday," the coach said. "If you took your eye off old Jack for a half a second he'd spurt past you. Furlong is the same way."

Manuel Guerrero, forward, Gordon Carpenter of the Phillips Oilers and Donald scored 17 for the Argentines.

Barksdale of the Oakland (Calif.) Bittners were America's leading scorers with 12 points each. Groza followed with 11.

Browning used ten men, the Olympic limit. He wasn't able to call on seven-foot Bob Kurland, the Phillips' scoring ace, when things got tough. Kurland was held out along with Jesse Renick of Phillips and the University of Kentucky's Cliff Barker and Ralph Beard.

The United States coach has been mixing up the squad in preliminary contest. When the championship flight begins, he plans to use the Oilers national A.A.U. champions from Bartlesville, Okla., and Kentucky College Kings as units.

Browning attributed the close squeeze to a series of mistakes and to the unexpectedly good showing of the opposition.

The triumph was the third for the United States in the round robin competition. The team has yet to play Peru and Egypt, two of the weaker members of Group C.

It was Argentina's first defeat, but the South Americans may get another shot at the United States squad. Two teams in each group qualify for the eight-team championship tournament.

U. S. 59

Player	FG	FT	Pts
Vince Boryla	2	1	5
Wallace Jones	1	2	4
Lewis Beck	1	0	2
Robert Robinson	2	0	4
Alex Groza	5	1	11
Don Barksdale	4	4	12
Ken Rollins	0	3	3
Ray Lumpp	1	2	4
R.C. Pitts	1	0	2
Gordon Carpenter	4	4	12
Totals	**21**	**17**	**59**

Argentina 57

Player	FG	FT	Pts
Juan Carlos Uder	3	0	6
Manuel Guerrero	6	5	17
Rafael Lledo	0	0	0
Oscar Furlong	4	10	18
Leopoldo "Pichon" Contarbio	0	1	1
Ricardo Primitivo Gonzalez	3	4	10
Tomas Vio	2	1	5
Calianeo	0	0	0
Totals	**18**	**21**	**57**

The U. S. team had things much easier in their fourth game, defeating Egypt 66-28. As reported in the Lexington Herald:

Peru Last Foe of U.S. Cagers Before Elimination Contests

LONDON, Aug. 5 (UP) -- The United State's mighty basketball squad, allowed by the schedule to rest today after playing three games in three days, is assured of a place in the Olympic elimination tournament next week and is certain to play at least two more games in Harringay arena.

Most followers of the sport feel the Yankee hoopsters are practically sure to appear in four more contests, winning all and capturing the Olympic basketball championship.

Coming back after being given a 59-57 scare the day before by Argentina, the U.S. squad dealt a 66-28 licking Wednesday night to Egypt, clinching a place and at least one appearance in the elimination affair. Its next foe will be Peru, to be faced Friday in the final round of the preliminary round-robin tourney.

The U.S. and probably Argentina will qualify from Group C to each of the other sections for next week's elimination play-off.

Mexico of Group D, one of the two other outfits undefeated at the start of today's competition, clinched a berth for next week with a 68-27 walloping of Iran in today's first game, the Cabelleros' fourth straight triumph.

The U.S. representative displayed a finer brand of ball as they conquered Egypt without difficulty.

The starting team, composed of Kurland, Renick, Pitts, Robinson and Barksdale, scored promptly after the opening jump and forged into a lead of 21-7 before being relieved by a quintet composed of Boryla, Jones, Lumpp, Barker and Beard.

The latter combination, starting the second half with a margin of 32-10, was in turn relieved late in the game by the original U.S. team with the count standing 52-25. Barksdale had played in the second array in the second half in place of Boryla.

U. S. 66

Player	FG	FT	FTA	PF	Pts
Robert Robinson	0	1	1	0	1
R.C. Pitts	1	2	2	0	4
Bob Kurland	6	3	4	4	15
Don Barksdale	6	5	6	1	17
Jesse Renick	1	0	0	0	2
Vince Boryla	3	3	4	4	9
Wallace Jones	3	0	0	3	6
Ray Lumpp	3	2	2	2	8
Ralph Beard	0	1	1	1	1
Cliff Barker	1	1	2	2	3
Totals	**24**	**18**	**22**	**17**	**66**

Egypt 28

Player	FG	FT	FTA	PF	Pts
Abdelrahman Ismail Hafez	1	0	0	4	2
Armand Philippe "Gaby" Catafago	0	2	4	4	2
Hussein Kamel Montasser	4	2	4	2	10
Fouad Abdel Meguid Abu El Kheir	0	0	1	1	0
Medat Youssef Mohamad	0	2	3	0	2
Yoessef Kamal Mohamed Abo-Ouf	1	4	4	4	6
Hassan Moawad	0	0	2	2	0
Ahmed Nessin	0	0	0	3	0
Mohamed Soliman	1	2	2	1	4
Robert Makzoume	1	0	0	0	2
Totals	**8**	**12**	**20**	**21**	**28**

The U. S. road to the gold continued with another rout, as reported in the New York Times:

U.S. FIVE DEFEATS PERUVIANS, 61-33

Wins fifth Straight to Reach Title Flight - Will Oppose Uruguay on Monday

LONDON, Aug 6 (AP) -- The United States basketball team rolled into the Olympic championship tournament today by defeating Peru, 61-33 , and immediately drew Uruguay as a first-round opponent.

The rangy, sharpshooting Yankees won five straight games to finish with a perfect record in the round-robin eliminations. Uruguay won three and lost two.

The game with Peru was marked by politeness on both sides and the Americans, who in the past had been subject to frequent booing on the part of the fans, actually received some cheers.

Coach Omar (Bud) Browning, the United States head mentor, had given instructions to his boys to make this one especially clean, and his proteges responded. They gave one of the smoothest exhibitions of ball handling, minus bodily contact, seen in the tournament to date. Nobody fouled out.

The assistant coach, University of Kentucky's Adolph Rupp, said that he had told the athletes to "quit this rough and rugged stuff and get out there and play slick like you do at home."

Wallace (Wah Wah) Jones, Kentucky guard, led the point making with a dozen counters. He was followed by Don Barksdale of the Oakland

(Calif.) Bittners, who tallied ten, and Ken Rollins of Kentucky, who scored nine.

Louis Beck of the Phillips (Okla.) Oilers and Kentucky's Alex Groza flipped in eight each.

Browning used the college members of the squad in the first half and the A.A.U. men in the second.

U. S. 61

Player	FG	FT	Pts
Ken Rollins	4	1	9
Ralph Beard	0	0	0
Don Barksdale	5	0	10
Gordon Carpenter	3	0	6
Alex Groza	3	2	8
Bob Kurland	1	0	2
Wallace Jones	6	0	12
Robert Robinson	1	0	2
Lewis Beck	4	0	8
Jesse Renick	2	0	4
Totals	**29**	**3**	**61**

Peru 33

Player	FG	FT	Pts
Virgilio Drago Burga	5	0	10
Alberto Fernandez Calderon	1	1	3
A. Ferreyos Perez	4	2	10
Jose Vicarra Nieto	0	1	1
G. Ahrens Valdivia	0	0	0
Rodolfo Salas Crespo	2	1	5
Luis Sanchez Maquiavelo	1	2	4
Carlos Alegre Benavides	0	0	0
Totals	**13**	**7**	**33**

The U. S. bandwagon rolled on against Uruguay, as reported by Benjamin Welles, New York Times:

U.S. QUINTET ROUTS URUGUAY BY 63-28

Mexico, France and Brazil Also Reach Semi-Final Round in Title Basketball

Special to the Times

LONDON, Aug. 9 -- The United States Olympic Basketball team entered the semi-final round here today by handing the Uruguayan combination a resounding defeat, 63 to 28.

At the same time, Mexico advanced with a 43 to 32 victory over Korea. France outmaneuvered a game Chilean five in overtime by the narrow margin of 53 to 52 to take her place in the penultimate round and Brazil, by virtue of a 28 to 23 triumph over Czechoslovakia, completed the foursome that will fight for places in the final.

The most exciting match of the day was that between France and Chile. From the opening whistle, the rival quintets went at top speed with both sides depending less on clever dribbling and fast footwork than on long overhead passes and slam-bang operations under the baskets.

In fact, France was behind most of the way and tied the score as the final bell sounded. The French sank one free throw for the winning point during the five minutes extra time.

France is now the sole European challenger for the title. Neither Mexico nor Brazil displayed championship class and the United States quintet is strongly favored to take the world honors.

A touch of color and music enlivened the otherwise drab proceedings at Harringay Arena when Brazilian rooters broke into dancing and singing after their team's victory. The sound of squealing clarinets and the sight of husky Brazilians in a conga line down the aisles intrigued the sober Brattiest spectators.

In a fast-moving match that saw one Uruguayan player collide with D.A. Barksdale of the United States team, necessitating the South American's removal on a stretcher, the United States five gradually wore down their opponents and won easily.

The North Americans' style, speed and stamina began to pay off early and near the end goals were dropping in the Uruguayan basket faster and faster.

Outstanding for the victors were R.A. Kurland, who scored 19 points; J.B. Renick, 10 points, and A.J. Groza, also with 10.

U. S. 63

Player	FG	FT	FTA	PF	Pts
Lewis Beck	3	1	1	1	7
R.C. Pitts	2	2	2	2	6
Bob Kurland	8	3	4	2	19
Don Barksdale	1	1	1	3	3
Jesse Renick	4	2	2	1	10
Vince Boryla	1	0	2	0	2
Ken Rollins	2	0	1	1	4
Cliff Barker	0	0	0	2	0
Alex Groza	4	2	2	2	10
Ralph Beard	1	0	0	0	2
Totals	**26**	**11**	**15**	**14**	**63**

Uruguay 28

Player	FG	FT	FTA	PF	Pts
Roberto Lovera	2	0	1	2	4
Hector Ruiz	0	1	1	0	1
Adesio Lombardo	5	4	10	3	14
Victorio Cieslinskas	0	0	0	2	0
Miguel Carlos Diab Figoli	1	1	1	0	3
Martin Acosta y Lara	1	0	3	1	2
Hector Garcia Otero	1	2	4	3	4
Neston F. Anton Giudice	0	0	0	2	0
Totals	**10**	**8**	**20**	**13**	**28**

It seemed only a matter of time for the U. S. as they rolled on in Game Seven, as reported by Allison Danzig, New York Times:

United States Routs Mexico

KENTUCKIANS PACE 71-TO-40 TRIUMPH

Groza Scores 19 U.S. Points Against Mexican Quintet -- Referee Evicts Kurland

FRENCH TRIP BRAZIL, 43-33

Special to The New York Times

LONDON, Aug. 11 -- The American basketball team hurdled what had been fancied the biggest obstacle in its path to the Olympic championship with a crushing victory over Mexico, 71 to 40, to reach the final round tonight. In the other semi-final, France unexpectedly defeated Brazil, 43 to 33, and will play the United States Friday night for the title in an intercontinental final.

An American victory is looked upon as a foregone conclusion to add to our sweeping triumphs in men's track and field and swimming and diving, as well as eight-oared rowing.

For the first time in the tournament, Head Coach Omar (Bud) Browning and his assistant, Adolph Rupp, elected to send out one of their two teams intact instead of using a scrambled line-up comprising chiefly Phillips Oilers and University of Kentucky players. Rupp's Wildcats were called on to start and it was not until well in the second half that seven-foot Bob Kurland saw action, although other Oilers had got into the contest earlier.

The expectation is that the Phillips 66 team, which won the National Amateur Athletic Union title for the seventh time this year and defeated Kentucky's National Collegiate Athletic Association champions in the final of the Olympic tryout tournament at Madison Square Garden, will get the call at the opening whistle in the final.

Alex Groza, Wallace (Wah Wah) Jones, Ralph Beard, Cliff Barker and Ken Rollins formed the starting line-up tonight and for the first ten minutes had a fight on their hands. The boys from across the Rio Grande, who entered the game unbeaten, showed a complete lack of respect for the fame of the Americans. Comparing favorably in height with their rivals, except for Groza and Jones, the Mexicans were so aggressive and fast and had so good an eye for the basket that the crowd in Harringay Arena was whipped up to a high state of excitement.

Mexico was first to score, dropping in a goal from the field immediately. After Jones had equalized and Barker had counted on a free throw, the lads from across the border went ahead again with a long set shot by Captain Santos de Leon, who was to give a good account of himself throughout.

The Kentuckians were not playing well, possibly because they were not quite sure of what the Italian and Egyptian officials expected. Unsettled at the start, they were uncertain and ragged in their combination play and could not locate the basket, particularly Beard.

Then the Americans found themselves and they moved with such speed, precision and cleverness in their passing that there was no stopping them. Big 6-foot 7-inch Groza was unbeatable in working with Jones and Beard in their fast-breaking set play which had ruined the opposition so many times during the American season.

From 6 to 5, the United States swept ahead to 13 to 5 with Groza laying them up and Barker and Jones also counting. Then Barker, racing down the court to take a pass under the basket, crashed into the backstop and his nose struck something hard, probably a two by four that was not properly padded.

Blood flowed from his nose which he had broken during the winter season, and Jesse Renick of the Oilers went in to take his place, the only new man Browning sent in during the first half. Whether the injury upset the Americans or the Mexicans took courage when Barker left the floor, the complexion of the game turned.

From a 13-6 deficit, Mexico pulled up to 13 to 12, Acuna Lizana throwing in two rather long one-handers that drew roars from the crowd. Again it looked as if a tight, hard-fought game was in prospect.

To this point is was definitely the best contest of the tournament with the Mexicans playing the game with a standard that most closely approximated that of the Americans. Argentina had held the United States to a 59-57 margin early in the tournament but the South Americans had not shown skill and speed to equal that of the Mexicans.

Our good neighbors and the crowd were speedily disillusioned if they entertained any idea that an American defeat might be in the making. From that point, Groza and Jones took charge on the offense and tallies soon followed one another so quickly that it soon became apparent that the only question was the ultimate score. Groza was always there for rebounds.

The Mexicans not only were unable to cope with the speed and accuracy of the United States' quick-breaking offense, but the American man-to-man defense was so effective that rival players could not get close to the basket. They were going for corners and shooting from far out and they were not hitting.

At half-time, the United States led, 30 to 14. When play was resumed, the same line-up was sent out that had finished the first half. Barker had re-entered the game in the last few minutes of the opening session as relief for Jones and he remained to begin the second half.

The Americans quickly increased their lead to 35 to 14 and then substitutes began to make their appearance. Ray Lumpp of New York University went in for Renick and was followed by Lew Beck and Gordon Carpenter of the Oilers.

The American attack continued in high gear as Beard found his eye and got into the scoring. Mexico did not score a field goal from the time it shot three in a row following the exit of Barker until near the middle of the second half.

With the score 48 to 25, Kurland went in for Groza. With all eyes on him, the big fellow scored on a free throw and then from the floor on a follow-up shot.

After tallying on two more layups, Foothills ran into a rival and sent him to the floor. Instantly there were boos and although there had been no intent on Kurland's part to injure his opponent, who jumped up unhurt, the referee took the rather high-handed action of sending him out of the game.

That gave an opportunity to Groza to re-enter and add to his total. As a result, the big Kentuckian displaced the Phillips giant as high scorer of the tournament. Tallying 19 points, Groza raised his total to 65, against 61 for Kurland, who accounted for 10, as also did Jones. Lizana was high man for Mexico with 9, followed by De Leon with 8.

France's victory over favored Brazil in the other semi-final was marked by scenes of wild excitement. The winning players hugged and kissed one another and danced in their joy while their countrymen in the stands cheered madly. Play became rough in the concluding stages, when the game was stopped a number of times and penalties inflicted.

U. S. 71

Player	FG	FT	FTA	PF	Pts
Cliff Barker	2	2	4	3	6
Wallace Jones	4	2	3	3	10
Ray Lumpp	1	3	4	3	5
Bob Kurland	4	2	3	3	10
Alex Groza	9	1	3	3	19
Gordon Carpenter	3	2	3	2	8
Jesse Renick	1	3	4	4	5
Ralph Beard	3	0	0	0	6
Ken Rollins	0	0	0	1	0
Lewis Beck	0	2	3	0	2
Totals	**27**	**17**	**27**	**22**	**71**

Mexico 40

Player	FG	FT	FTA	PF	Pts
Jose Rojas Herrara	1	4	5	4	6
Isaac Alfara Loza	0	0	0	2	0
Alberto Bienvenu Bajaras	0	0	0	2	0
Jose Santos de Leon	3	2	2	3	8
Cardiel	0	2	2	0	2
Gudino	1	4	5	2	6
R. Rojas	0	2	2	4	2
Angel Acuna Lizana	4	1	3	1	9
Diaz	1	2	3	0	4
Guerrrero	1	1	5	3	3
Totals	**11**	**18**	**27**	**21**	**40**

The U. S. finished off the tournament with a gold medal triumph, as described by Benjamin Welles, New York Times:

AMERICAN QUINTET TRIUMPHS BY 65-21

Entire Oiler-Kentucky Team Sees Action -- French Trail at Half-Time by 28-9

Special to The New York Times

LONDON, Aug. 13 -- America's highly-touted basketball team swamped a hard-fighting French quintet in Harringay Arena tonight by a score of 65 to 21 to capture the Olympic laurel wreath in token of the world championship.

By crushing the French team the United States not only retained the title gained at Berlin in the 1936 games, but re-emphasized American world superiority in this particular brand of athletics.

Unprecedented in a championship match was the International Federation's permission for both teams to use their entire contingent as substitutes. The Federation waived the normal ruling limiting the teams to five playing members and five substitutes.

The American team took the lead at the start and quickly began to outmaneuver, outdribble and outshoot the French players, many of whom had learned the fine points of the game from Americans stationed in France during the war.

The crowd, estimated at 6,000 was one of the largest ever to view a basketball contest in Britain.

Brazil beat Mexico, 52 to 47, in an exciting match for third and fourth places. The Brazilians, who were behind, 17 to 25, at the half, came back in brilliant style and at the end Brazilian rooters and officials raced onto the court hugging and kissing the players.

U. S. (65) Player	FG	FT	FTA	PF	Pts
Lewis Beck	2	2	2	0	6
R.C. Pitts	3	1	1	0	7
Vince Boryla	1	1	1	1	3
Robert Robinson	1	0	0	2	2
Ralph Beard	1	2	2	0	4
Ray Lumpp	5	0	1	0	10
Bob Kurland	2	0	0	0	4
Don Barksdale	3	2	3	2	8
Alex Groza	5	1	1	3	11
Gordon Carpenter	0	2	2	1	2
Jesse Renick	1	0	0	0	2
Ken Rollins	1	0	0	0	2
Wallace Jones	1	2	2	2	4
Cliff Barker	0	0	2	1	0
Totals	**26**	**13**	**17**	**12**	**65**

Mexico (21) Player	FG	FT	FTA	PF	Pts
Fernand Guillon	0	1	1	0	1
Jacques Pierrier	2	1	2	4	5
Andre Even	0	0	0	0	0
Yvan Quenin	0	0	0	0	0
Maurice Girardot	0	0	1	0	0
Maurice De Saymonnet	0	0	0	1	0
Rene Derency	0	1	1	2	1
Piere Thiolin	1	1	4	1	3
Andre Buffiere	0	0	1	3	0
Rene Chocat	3	2	2	2	8
Raymond Offner	1	0	0	0	2
Lucien Rebuffic	0	1	1	0	1
Andre Barrais	0	0	0	0	0
Totals	**7**	**7**	**13**	**13**	**21**

CHAPTER 3

First Success, Then Comes the Gamblers

After Kentucky's fantastic 1947-48 season, Coach Rupp found himself with several thousand dollars left over from the UK-Oilers exhibition games and fan donations sent in to help the Wildcats defray costs for sending extra players on their Olympics trip.

In December 1948 Coach Rupp met in his office with Coach Lancaster to discuss what to do with the money.

"Harry, the fans sent this in for the boys and I think it should go to the boys," said Coach Rupp.

"I agree, coach, but I don't know how we can do it, legally or within the rules, I mean," said Lancaster.

"Why don't we just dole it out throughout the season, giving the boys $20 here and there, and maybe sometimes $50, if they have played well?" said Rupp.

"Well, a lot of the guys – like Beak and Beard – could sure use the dough, with their family situations and all," said Lancaster.

"Let's do it that way, then," said Rupp. "But I will check with (UK) president (Herman) Donovan to make sure it's legal before we do it."

Donovan gave Rupp and Lancaster the OK to distribute the money to the players. Donovan compared Kentucky's trip to the Sugar Bowl hoops tournament in New Orleans as the same thing as a football trip to a bowl game, where football players were legally given extra spending money. UK basketball players received up to $50 each spending money at the Sugar Bowl tournament. This was a decision that would later come back to haunt the school.

As the season progressed several players, including Groza and Beard, found themselves handed $20 bills by Rupp and

Lancaster from the Olympics leftover cash after good play.

With their national and international success Kentucky became high on the list of basketball games featured by gamblers as the 1948-49 season continued.

The betting line each week featured Kentucky and whoever they happened to be playing. Millions of dollars changed hands every week.

Kentucky did not have strong security for its players. Access to the UK dressing room was fairly easy as fans and well-wishers often flocked in.

After a mid-December 1948 win over Arkansas, in which Beard scored 15 points, he found himself shaking hands with Nick "The Greek" Englisis, a New York City guy who had come to UK on a football scholarship. But Coach Bryant had upgraded the football talent at UK and Englisis was left far down the bench. He quit the team and somehow became an assistant UK basketball team manager.

"Great game, Ralph," said Englisis, sticking out his hand.

When Beard shook his hand he suddenly found himself holding a $20 bill.

"What the hell is this all about, Greek," said Beard.

"Just a little token of gratitude from Ed Curd and the boys downtown," said Englisis.

"Gratitude for w-w-what?" said Beard.

"Well, you guys more than upheld the point spread and Ed and his friends made quite a few bucks on the game," said Englisis.

Beard was puzzled. "Thanks, I guess, but I s-s-still don't understand."

"Just relax and enjoy it. Buy yoself sump'n nice," said Englisis, moving away to Groza's locker, where he shook hands with him, also palming a $20 bill off to him.

"Hey, thanks, Greek," said Groza. "You hit a winner at the race track?"

Englisis gave Groza the same spiel and moved over to Barnstable's locker, where he did the same thing.

After Englisis left, Beard, Groza and Barnstable huddled quietly at Beard's locker.

"Looks like we made some people happy, huh, guys," said Groza.

"Yeah, without even trying," said Barnstable. "Guess there's nothing wrong if somebody wants to give us money for no reason. And Coach Rupp and Coach Lancaster have rewarded us with a little money from time to time, so I guess we ought to just relax and enjoy it."

"Still, I don't think w-w-we need to be talking about this with the other fellas, since we don't know if Greek gave them some money, too," said Beard.

"Yeah, you're right, Ralph, no need to get things stirred up," said Groza.

After handing out several $20 bills and $50 bills to Groza, Beard and Barnstable as the 1948-49 season progressed, Curd and Englisis approached the trio about making even more money.

The gamblers met with the trio of UK players in the dining room of the Phoenix Hotel in downtown Lexington in January 1949.

"You boys have been real good at beating the point spread," said Curd, unfolding a napkin on his lap as the five sat looking over the menu.

"Dinner is on me boys – have anything you like," said Curd. "Desert, too,"

"Ya hear that, Ralph – you can even have ice cream," said Groza, laughing.

"I don't get it . . . what's so funny," said Englisis, smiling inquisitively.

"It's sort of an inside joke," said Groza. "(Assistant) Coach (Harry) Lancaster told Ralph one day that he needed to lighten up a little, that he was overdoing his training workouts. He told him he ought to go out and break training rules every once in a while. So, Ralph went out and bought himself a gallon of ice cream and ate it all by himself."

Everybody laughed except Beard. "Is it a crime to l-l-like ice cream?" he said.

"Hell, no," said Curd. "Have yourself all the ice cream you want tonight."

The players took advantage of the free meal as they all ordered steak.

As everyone was finishing up their desserts – Ralph was having ice cream with chocolate syrup topping – Curd got down to business.

"Boys, you may or may not know I work with some big-time gamblers out of New York City, including Frankie Costello," said Curd. "These guys usually use me to make basketball bets for them. You guys have been good at winning games over the point spread. Now we are asking that you not beat the spread – win, but win less than the point spread calls for. For example if you are favored by 12 points, win by 11 or less."

"So, you are asking us to make sure we don't run away from teams – keep the games closer," said Groza.

"Exactly. We stand to make more money by you winning under the point spread than by going over the spread," said Englisis.

"We are not asking for you to throw games," said Curd. "I know you guys would never do that. We are just asking you to control the winning margin."

"B-b-but wouldn't that probably hurt some UK fans who bet on us to b-b-beat teams more than the point spread?" said Beard.

"Maybe a few," said Curd. "But the big-money betting is done in the larger cities, particularly New York, Boston, Philadelphia, Chicago. I don't think we have many big betters in Lexington, Louisville or the rest of the state. Besides, we don't want you to hold down the score for every game – just a few here and there. I'm a friend of Coach Rupp . . . I wouldn't want anything bad to happen to him or you guys."

"So, what kind of money are we talking about – I mean, for us," said Groza.

"Anywhere from a couple hundred up to a couple of thousand – each," said Curd.

"Are you talking to any other UK players," said Groza, "Wah Wah in particular?"

"No," said Curd, "we figure you three are enough to control things. And we feel Wah Wah would just not be cooperative."

"I think we n-n-need to talk about this among ourselves," said Beard.

"I agree," said Groza. "Give us a day or two and we will let you know what we decide."

The next day Beard, Groza and Barnstable met at their athletic dorm.

"I don't know what you guys think," said Beard. "But I don't like doing anything that might hurt UK fans. They have been very loyal to us and I don't want to cost them m-m-money. I don't mind so much getting money for winning games over the point spread. That is just getting paid to play good ball. But it's a different deal trying to hold the score under the point spread. That means we would sometimes have to deliberately play bad and I don't l-l-like that idea at all. I have too much pride to deliberately screw up."

"I agree," said Groza. "But, like Mr. Curd said, we are talking about only small amounts of betting money by UK fans – and it would only involve a few games. It's not like we were actually throwing games. We would still win, and that's the main thing."

"No real harm, the way I see it," said Barnstable. "It's not like we are doing anything illegal. People who bet are the ones breaking the law. The only ones who stand a chance of getting hurt bad are the gamblers."

"And, I guess it's not so bad. Coach has been giving us some money, too, for playing good," Groza told Beard.

So, the Wildcats trio agreed to accept money for going over the spread in several games during the 1948-49 season.

The players agreed to play over the point spread in a 56-45 win over DePaul and a 72-50 win over Vanderbilt. On February 8, 1949, the players agreed for the first time to play under the point spread. Kentucky did win the game against Tennessee 71-56, three points under the 18-point betting line. Groza scored 34 points in that game.

After one home game in February 1949 Coach Rupp saw Curd in the UK dressing room talking to some of his players.

"What's that guy doing in here?" Rupp said to Lancaster. "Get him out of here. I don't want bookies in our locker room."

"I let him in when Beak told me that Curd had told him he was a friend of yours," said Lancaster.

"He's no friend of mine," said Rupp. "I have met him a few times at parties and he made a donation to our Shriner's Hospital fund drive, but you know how I feel about gamblers. Make sure he does not get in here again."

Rupp had been adamantly opposed to the idea of gambling on sports events and had criticized newspapers for printing point spread information.

The players had each received about $700 from Curd as the 1948-49 season progressed.

Beard continued to visit his mother regularly and kept giving her the money he received from the point-shaving.

His mother became suspicious on one of Ralph's home visits.

"I don't understand how you can get this much money, Ralph. "You are not stealing it, are you? – you know I would never stand for that. I would rather starve to death than steal from another person," she told him.

"No, m-m-mom, I am not stealing it. I am earning it," he told her.

"How are you earning it – do you have a job at school?" she asked.

"Yeah, sort of," he said. "I just kind of help manage the basketball team -- y'know, take care of a lot of little things."

"Well, just make sure you stay out of trouble," she said. "I raised you as an honest boy and I want you to stay that way."

Beard swallowed hard when his mom confronted him with that statement.

He, too, detested the idea of helping gamblers make money by using the players, but times were hard and he felt being able to help his mother overrode his concerns.

Kentucky had rolled along to a 29-1 record entering the post-season NIT tournament in New York City in March of

1949. The team's only defeat was a 42-40 loss to St. Louis on Dec. 30 in the finals of the Sugar Bowl tournament in New Orleans.

No Wildcats did any point-shaving in that game. It was apparently just a matter of them having an off night against a good basketball team.

"Podnah, that game really hurt," Beard told Groza as the team travelled back to Lexington. "St. Louis is a g-g-good team but we could beat them 99 out of a hundred times."

"Yeah, no doubt," said Groza. "But we just got to suck it up and go on. We still need to win the NIT and the NCAA. No team has ever done that in the same season. We need to be the first."

The Wildcats did not lose another regular season game and a couple of months later the Big Blue were getting ready to travel to New York City, where they faced the Loyola Ramblers of Chicago in the first round of the NIT.

Curd met with Beard, Groza and Barnstable at the Phoenix Hotel dining room the night before the team was to leave for New York City.

"Boys, since this game is going to be played in New York City, Costello is going to be laying down some big money," said Curd. "We need your help. You are 11-point favorites. We are going to give each of you $2,000 to hold the game down so you don't win by more than 10 points. There's a lot of money being laid down on you winning by more than 11. We are laying a lot of dough on the under the point spread."

Groza whistled. "Wow -- two grand. That's our biggest payday ever."

"We should w-w-win easily," said Beard. "But it might be tough to try to play the game that close."

The three took the money and later got together at the athletic dorm to discuss what they needed to do.

"If we get too far ahead, then we need to make some turnovers, miss some shots and play poor defense so Loyola can cut it to ten or less," said Groza. "Don'tcha agree, Barney?"

"Yeah, but we don't want to make it look too obvious," said Barnstable. "The best way to keep the score down is to play poor defense."

"Damn, I really hate doing this," said Beard. "I don't think I can force myself to deliberately screw up. It's just not in my nature. If we get too far ahead, you guys will have to try to bring the score back down."

"Well, if we only have a few minutes left and we need to cut the score back down, you just kind of stay out of the offense," said Barnstable. "And ease up a little on defense."

But Loyola was not a top 20 team (the tournament's lowest seed, 16th) and UK under normal circumstances would not have a tough time beating them soundly.

CHAPTER 4:

A Point Spread Deal Goes Awry

      The Wildcat trio was not up to their normal level of play as the Loyola game got underway before 12,592 fans at Madison Square Garden on Monday afternoon, March 14, 1949.

      Here's how the game went, according to a story in the Lexington Herald by sports writer Babe Kimbrough:

NEW YORK, March 14 -- Kentucky's dream of winning two national basketball tourneys -- a feat never accomplished by a college quintet -- turned into a nightmare here this afternoon as the Wildcats dropped their first National Invitation engagement to Loyola of Chicago, 67-56, in Madison Square Garden.

A matinee crowd of 12,592 fans saw the Ramblers, a fighting quintet without too much finesse, battle the once-feared Kentuckians of Coach Adolph Rupp on even terms for 32 minutes and then forge to the front to pull the greatest cage upset of the year.

Although the Wildcats were well off on their shooting, missing many easy layups and set shots from out on the court, it was not their poor marksmanship from the field that dragged them down in defeat. It was at the free-throw line that Loyola won its glory.

Each team chalked up 21 field goals during the afternoon but the Ramblers sank 25 charity shots out of 34 attempts while the Cats were connecting for 14 out of 22. Strange as it might seem, the Kentuckians had 29 personals called on them as compared with 19 for the Chicago cagers.

When the battle ended, Coach Rupp had all of his "height" sitting on the bench beside him, Alex Groza, Wallace (Wah Wah) Jones and Walt Hirsch having been ousted by free-whistling Officials Matty Begovich and Jammy Moskowitz. Jones was the first to go out with nine and a half minutes of playing time remaining.

Then Groza followed him with four minutes and 45 seconds left and Hirsch trotted to the sideline 25 seconds later.

It was the same old Madison Square Garden story. At the end of the first period, when the Wildcats were trailing, 32-31, Jones, Dale Barnstable and Groza each had three personal fouls on them and Hirsch had four.

Jack Kerris, star center for the Ramblers, had four, too, but he lasted out the final period without accumulating another as the Kentuckians paraded to the bench.

Immediately after the game, Coach Rupp announced that the Kentucky team would return to Lexington Tuesday by plane so the players could attend classes for the remainder of the week before coming back to New York to face Villanova next Monday in the first round of the Eastern Division of the National Collegiate Athletic Association tournament.

Drawings in the NCAA were announced today. Illinois and Yale will tie up in the first tilt on next Monday's program, with the Cats and Villanova playing the second game.

Before today's battle, experts who had seen Kerris in action warned that he was a tough ball player and he proved to be just that. Making good use of a well-

developed hook shot, he collected seven field goals and nine charity tosses to lead both quintets in scoring with a total of 23.

Groza, who had broken practically every scoring record in the Southeastern Conference this season, was limited to 12 points -- all made in the first half -- and relinquished high-scoring honors for the Cats to little Ralph Beard, who tallied 15.

The veteran Cliff Barker, who was outstanding for the Blue Grass five, both in floor work and shooting, equaled Groza's total with 12 points on five field goals and a pair of free throws.

This afternoon's loss by the Wildcats left the state of Kentucky without a representative in the Invitation tourney, Western's Hilltoppers having dropped a 95-86 decision to the Bradley University Braves in the first game of the day's program after holding a 50-45 advantage at the half.

There was never a time that the Ruppmen flashed the championship form that has been theirs as they sailed through the regular season with but a single loss -- to St. Louis in the Sugar Bowl -- and the SEC tournament in Louisville.

From the very beginning they lacked the fire which has characterized their play and were unable to chalk up enough consecutive points to see daylight. Time and again they took the ball down the floor, missed a shot and then lost the rebound to the rampaging Ramblers. They seemed always to be in the wrong place when the ball came bounding off the boards.

Loyola took a quick lead when Gerry Nagel connected with a long shot from the side of the court and Kerris followed with one of his special hooks. Finally, however, the Wildcats by hard work and some luck managed to pull in front to hold an 8-5 advantage at the end of five minutes of play.

From there on out it was nip-and-tuck through the first period. In the next five minutes the score was knotted at 9-9, 11-11, 14-14, 16-16, 17-17 before the Kentuckians managed to ease to a one-point advantage at 18-17 midway of the half.

But the Ramblers quickly tied it up at 18-18 on a free throw by Ralph Klaerick and then went ahead on another gratis shot by the same performer.

The count was knotted again at 20-20. Then the Cats took a three-point lead, only to have the Chicagoans comes back and tie it up again. It was all even at 23-23 and 25-25.

Kentucky went to the front again at 30-27 but Loyola tallied five points in succession to steal the advantage again while the Wildcats were collecting a single point before the intermission.

As the second half started, Blue Grass fans took on new hope when the Ruppmen tallied three straight fielders, two by Jones and one by Beard.

However, the Ramblers began to amble again and at the end of five minutes had sliced the Cats' advantage to one point, at 38-37. Midway of the second period the scoreboard showed the teams even again at 47-47, but a long shot by Beard and a free throw by Jim Line put the Cats back on top. However, the Kentucky guns were silent while Loyola chalked up six points.

With the clock showing five minutes remaining, the Kentuckians had clipped Loyola's lead to three points, at 57-54. A minute later it was down to two points at 58-56 when Line made good a pair of free shots.

But with Line's effort, the book was closed on Kentucky and the Ramblers became the giant-killers of the tournament for in the last four minutes the Wildcats failed to tally while Loyola hung up nine points to widen its victory margin to 11.

The box score from the UK-Loyola game:

Kentucky 56

Player	FG	FT	FTA	PF	Pts
Wallace Jones	2	2	3	5	6
Jim Line	2	3	3	4	7
Dale Barnstable	1	2	4	3	4
Walter Hirsch	0	0	0	5	0
Alex Groza	5	2	5	5	12
Roger Day	0	0	0	2	0
Ralph Beard	6	3	3	1	15
Cliff Barker	5	2	4	4	12
Totals	21	14	22	29	56

Loyola 67

Player	FG	FT	FTA	PF	Pts
Ed Earle	3	3	4	3	9
Frank O'Grady	0	1	2	2	1
Ralph Klaerich	1	5	5	2	7
Ben Bluitt	3	3	4	0	9
Jack Kerris	7	9	12	4	23
Ed Dawson	1	0	0	1	2
Jim Nicholl	1	3	3	2	5
Art Hildebrand	0	0	0	3	0
Gerry Nagel	5	1	4	3	11
Totals	21	25	34	20	67

That night after the game Beard, Groza and Barnstable met in Beard's room at their New York City hotel.

Beard nearly broke out in tears as the trio discussed the game.

"Pahds, that w-w-was disgraceful. We let our fans down, we let ourselves down. We were thinking too much about the point s-s-spread than the game. It threw us off too much," said Beard.

"That, and the officiating, which I thought was terrible," said Barnstable. "They called a lot of dinky stuff on us and let them get away with murder. Beak, Wah Wah and Walter (Hirsch) all fouled out with lots of time still left on the clock. They did not have a single guy foul out."

"Ralph, it certainly was not your fault – you played great. The rest of us just kinda stunk up the game," said Groza. "That Kerris guy was a good player, but we have played against a lot better. The refs wouldn't let me touch him without calling a foul. I was deliberately playing kinda soft in the first half, but when it started looking like we might actually lose I started playing harder. But the refs were doing a sorry job and I fouled out."

"Yeah, I saw you crying on the bench," said Beard. "I felt like shit there at the end. I knew we had just screwed up terribly."

"I wonder if those big-time gamblers got to those refs, too," said Barnstable.

"I got to be a little suspicious of that, too, considering how one-sided the game was called," said Groza.

"I don't even want to talk to Curd or the Greek the rest of this season," said Beard. "We have g-g-got to make up for this game by playing well in the NCAA tournament. We don't need to have our minds c-c-cluttered up any more with point-shaving shit."

The three agreed they would not meet with Curd or Englisis the rest of the season.

Coach Rupp met with the news media after the game and was peppered with questions about his team's apparent underachieving.

"Coach, what do you think was wrong with your team today, since they appeared to be playing without a lot of enthusiasm and far below their normal game," asked a New York Times sportswriter.

"Well, I would certainly like to know the answer to that myself," said Rupp. Maybe they got blinded by the big city bright lights. They certainly looked like they were shooting like blind men out there today."

The media room roared with laughter.

"Coach, do you think you could beat Loyola if you played them again?" asked a Daily News sports writer.

"Fellas, I don't believe in what-if this or what-if that conjecture. The famous British writer William Hazlitt once said, 'You know more of a road by having traveled it than by all the conjectures and descriptions in the world.' Well we know a lot about the road we went down today. Unfortunately, we found out it was a dead-end."

"Coach, can you put this game behind you and come back to New York next week and play your normal game in the NCAA tournament?" said a New York Post sportswriter.

"Well, son, I never worry about tomorrow. We have suffered a great disappointment here today, but the world will not come to an end here today, because it's already tomorrow in Australia."

A writer asked Coach Rupp if he was upset about his team giving up too many easy baskets to Loyola and maybe he ought to put his lucky brown suit back in the closet.

"I told my boys that the Bible says it was better to give than receive. But it's better to be on the receiving end. The Bible also says says to love thine enemy. That's the old version. That was before Louisville, North Carolina, Indiana and Tennessee started playing basketball. Now you boys have started calling me The Man in the Brown Suit. Now back in the 1920s when I was coaching in high school in Illinois I had just one suit and it was brown. When I finally got enough money to buy a new one, I got myself a blue one. I wore it to a game and we got shellacked. I have been wearing brown ever since. I got about a dozen brown suits in my closet."

"Are you going to be working your boys overtime in practice because of their showing here today," said an NBC Radio reporter.

"Well, we've got to get these boys back to Lexington so they can go to their classes then we have a short turnaround to come back to New York City for the NCAA tournament. I will talk to my assistant coach, Harry Lancaster, and we will figure out how we should handle practices before the NCAA. I just don't believe in overworking your players right before a tournament. They need to have their legs – we don't want them out there playing heavy-legged. But I can tell you one thing for sure, they will be hearing a few well-chosen words from me about them playing with a little more enthusiasm. You can be the greatest salesman in the world, but without enthusiasm, you are just a clerk. We don't need clerks on our basketball team."

Later that evening Coach Rupp met with Coach Lancaster in his room at the team's hotel.

"Harry, I just don't understand what happened to our boys out there today. I know we did not get good officiating, but our team played very listlessly," said Rupp, sitting on the bed and looking at a stat sheet from the game.

Lancaster was sitting in a chair, also looking at a copy of the stat sheet.

"Hard to believe that Groza did not score in the second half," said Lancaster. "Course, he fouled out early in the second half. I'm of the opinion we need to run their asses off in Lexington – give 'em a wakeup call," said Lancaster.

"I don't want to do that, Harry. We need them to have their legs for the NCAA. I think they will be mad enough at themselves to want to make up for this damn fiasco."

But Rupp went against his own advice when the team got back to Lexington.

"I was so damn mad I just couldn't contain myself," said Rupp. "I put those boys through three days of hellacious, bloodthirsty, practices. We practiced like the Dickens, I'm telling you."

Rupp was still puzzled by his team's poor play against Loyola. He and Athletic Directory Bernie Shively were sitting in Rupp's office, sharing a fifth of whiskey the day before the team was due to leave for New York.

"I don't know, Bernie. But, Lordy I think there's something wrong with this team," said Rupp.

"Awwww, the Loyola game was just a one-in-a-million slipup, Adolph. They will be fine when they get back out there, I'm sure."

"I hope so, Bernie, because if we would lose two in a row people in Lexington will be hanging me in effigy downtown."

CHAPTER 5:

Cats Boot Gamblers, Win Second NCAA

Three days after returning to Lexington and after receiving a tongue-lashing from Coach Rupp at practice on Wednesday, Beard, Groza and Barnstable were meeting in Groza's room when there was a knock on their door.

Groza opened the door and found himself face to face with Curd and Englisis.

Curd pushed his way in past Groza.

"Sorry to see you boys lose like that in the NIT in New York," said Curd, "but sometimes things just get out of hand."

Beard rolled off Groza's bed, where he had been reclining, and used both hands to grab Curd by his suit coat collar.

"But I'll bet it didn't m-m-make your New York buddies unhappy," said Beard angrily. "Looks like you guys won your bets and we didn't even have anything to do with it. You didn't get your m-m-money's worth from us, now did you?"

Curd knocked his hand away and Groza grabbed Beard and made him sit down.

"Okay, boys, I know you are upset. But that was just one game and you have had a great season, with the NCAA still a big plum out there waiting on you," said Curd.

"So, what do you guys want?" said Barnstable.

Curd took out his billfold and pulled a big wad of hundred dollar bills from it.

"You guys can make some real money now if you have a mind to," said Curd. "These NCAA games will see a lot of heavy betting – maybe a million dollars or more. If you boys will go along with us, there will be thousands of dollars in it for you."

Beard's face flushed red with anger and he rushed toward Curd with his fists drawn, only to again be restrained by Groza and Barksdale.

"You b-b-bastard, I'll break your friggin' neck," said Beard, straining to pull himself away.

"Get the hell out of here," said Groza. "Don't ever speak to any of us again, or I'll personally help Ralph break your little crooked neck."

Curd and Englisis scurried away.

Beard, Groza and Barnstable did not hear from them for a few days but they were not ready to give up.

When Curd and Englisis showed up at the UK basketball dorm in mid-March 1949 they were greeted less than warmly.

They arrived at Groza's room, finding both Groza and Beard studying for classroom examinations.

Beard had opened the door and when he saw Curd and Englisis he slammed the door in their faces.

But Curd opened the door and stuck his foot inside to keep it from being slammed again.

"Don't get excited, boys, I'm just here to talk business," said Curd, forcing his way inside.

"We got no more business with you rats," said Beard. "Get the hell out."

"Now just a minute," said Curd. "Hear me out, will ya. I'm here to give you the offer of a lifetime. Now listen to this: We are prepared to offer you two and Barnstable $10,000 each to help us control the score in only two of your NCAA games."

"I wouldn't do that again for a f-f-ucking million dollars," said Beard.

"Me, neither," said Groza, "and I know that goes for Barney, too. You guys are not going to mess up our lives any more. If we had it to do over we would never have taken a dime from you bums."

"Don't be stupid, fellas," said Englisis. "You'll never get a chance like this again."

Beard started pushing Curd toward the door and Curd pulled out a pistol and started waving it at the players.

Beard caught Curd on the jaw with an overhand right, sending the burly gambler to the floor. He was out cold, the pistol lying at his side.

Beard, fists raised, angrily turned toward Englisis.

"Whoa . . . just a minute," said Englisis, holding up his hands in surrender. "I'm leaving, okay?"

"Take this piece of trash with you," said Groza, picking up Curd and placing him in Englisis' arms.

Groza stuck the pistol in Englisis' jacket pocket and Englisis with great difficulty carried the still unconscious Curd to his car, placed him in the back seat and drove away.

"That felt good," said Beard.

"Yeah – too bad we didn't do that last year," said Groza.

Curd regained consciousness as Englisis drove away from the UK campus.

"What the hell happened," said Curd, rubbing his jaw.

"Beard cold-cocked you," said Englisis. "I don't think we can do any more business with those guys."

"Yeah, well forget those bastards," said Curd. "But I gotta let the boys in New York know."

The next day Curd called Frankie Costello in New York.

"Frankie, we are not going to be able to do any more business with those Kentucky boys," said Curd.

"Whazza matter?" said Costello.

"They got religion, I guess. I went over yesterday to talk to them about the $10,000 offer and they kicked me out. The Beard kid just clocked me."

"Fuck, that's too bad," said Costello. "Can't you get any of their other players to cooperate?"

"The only other one who would be in a position to control the game is the Jones kid and I know he is too strait-laced for us to get on our team. I think we are out of luck with that team. At least for the rest of this season."

"Dammit, that could be a problem for us. But I know we got some of the Eastern teams guys working with us, including players at CCNY,

LIU and Long Island, so we can still make some good bucks," said Costello.

Meanwhile, Beard met with Groza and Barnstable.

When Barnstable was told what had happened, he gave Beard and Groza a hearty handshake.

"Thanks, guys, we need to steer clear of bastards like that," he said.

"Particularly if we ever hope to have a chance to play in the pros," said Groza.

"I just hope we haven't already ruined it for ourselves," said Beard.

"I think we will be okay," said Barnstable. "We never ever tanked a game. That Loyola game was the only one that really hurt us."

"Just pray that n-n-never comes back to haunt us," said Beard.

Englisis later told investigators he had tried to get UK players involved in the NCAA tournament point-shaving in 1949, but had been rebuffed.

He said Groza told him: "The little guy (Beard) and Barney (Barnstable) are worried about losing. . . and they're afraid somebody might get wise to what we've been doing."

Having rid themselves of the gamblers, the Wildcats rolled through the 1948-49 season in grand style, finishing 29-2 in the regular season.

The Wildcats returned to New York City for the NCAA tournament in March of 1949, beating No. 14 Villanova 85-72 and No. 4 Illinois 75-47 on March 21-22 in the Eastern Regional. They then flew to Seattle for the NCAA championship game, beating No. 2 Oklahoma State 46-36 on March 26, 1949.

Here's how the championship game was reported by the New York Times:

Groza Leads Kentucky to 2d N.C.A.A. Crown

SEATTLE, March 27, 1949 -- Back to the Bluegrass state goes the national collegiate basketball championship, which was won by a great University of Kentucky team that broke the heart of the fighting Oklahoma Aggies last night, 46-36.

A big, hulking bear of a man who moves with deceptive grace was the key to the Wildcats' victory.

When 6-foot-7 inch Alex Groza fouled out five minutes before the end of the game, he had poured in 25 points and carried Kentucky to its triumph on his burly shoulders.

There was no doubt in the minds of sportswriters who had watched the all-America senior center in action. They unanimously voted him the most valuable player award for the second straight National Collegiate Athletic Association tournament.

Before the title game, watched by a turn-away crowd of 12,500 at the University of Washington Pavilion, the Big Nine champions from Illinois had taken third place by defeating Pacific Coast Conference champion Oregon State, 57-53.

The jubilant Kentuckians, heading back by chartered plane today to Lexington, took with them half of basketball's double diadem for which they had been aiming.

Twelve days earlier, they lost their chance at a twin sweep in the National Invitation Tournament at New York, where they were rudely dumped on their press clippings by unawed Loyola of Chicago.

But in the roaring finish that carried them through the Eastern N.C.A.A. finals and the championship here, the Wildcats proved their No. 1 rating in the eyes of the fans.

After it was all over, beaming Coach Adolph Rupp said:

"It was a tough game all the way. We had to play this one the hard way, almost to the finish. We beat a good team and we're mighty happy about it."

The Aggie's coach, Hank Iba, shrugged off defeat with "We just had a bad night; we were way off on our shots."

But hitting or not, Oklahoma A&M would have still had that Groza edge to overcome. Fouls cost Groza his chance to crack the all-time N.C.A.A. single game scoring record of 31 set in 1941 by George Glamack of North Carolina. With four personals against him, Groza was benched for eight minutes in the second half, then got back in just past the midway mark and finally went out via the foul route five minutes before the gun.

Oklahoma A&M stepped off to a 5-2 lead with its ball-control style of play. The Groza started to roll. At the half it was 25-20 for Kentucky and the big guy had accounted for 15 points.

The Aggies' battle was lost when lanky Bob Harris, who matches Groza in height but is 28 pounds lighter at 198, was whistled to the sidelines with five personals early in the second half. Then near the end of the game A&M's scrappy J.L. Parks went out on fouls and it was all over. Kentucky stalled to the finish.

Kentucky 46

Player	FG	FT	FTA	PF	Pts
Wallace Jones	1	1	3	3	3
Cliff Barker	1	3	3	4	5
Jim Line	2	1	2	3	5
Alex Groza	9	7	8	5	25
Walter Hirsch	1	0	0	1	2
Ralph Beard	1	1	2	4	3
Dale Barnstable	1	1	1	1	3
Totals	**16**	**14**	**19**	**21**	**46**

Oklahoma A&M 36

Player	FG	FT	FTA	PF	Pts
Vernon Yates	1	0	0	1	2
Joe Bradley	0	3	5	3	3
Bob Harris	3	1	1	5	7
J.L. Parks	2	3	4	5	7
Jack Shelton	3	6	7	4	12
Tom Jaquet	0	1	2	0	1
Gale McArthur	0	2	2	1	2
Norman Pilgram	0	2	2	1	2
Keith Smith	0	0	0	1	0
Totals	**9**	**18**	**23**	**21**	**36**

The 1948-49 player statistics for the 32-2 UK team

Player	Games Played	FG	FGA	%	FT	FTA	%	F	Total Pts	PPG
Alex Groza	34	259	612	42.3	180	248	72.6	103	698	20.53
Ralph Beard	34	144	481	29.9	82	115	71.3	55	370	10.88
Wallace Jones	32	130	440	29.5	49	75	65.3	88	309	9.66
Cliff Barker	34	94	315	29.8	60	88	68.2	99	248	7.29
Dale Barnstable	34	84	309	27.2	41	57	71.9	79	209	6.15
Jim Line	32	70	195	35.9	43	51	84.3	67	183	5.72
Walter Hirsch	34	67	209	32.1	22	32	68.8	65	156	4.59
Roger Day	19	21	39	53.8	9	17	52.9	20	51	2.68
Al Bruno	9	9	30	30	2	3	66.7	8	20	2.22
Garland Townes	16	10	48	20.8	11	20	55	17	31	1.94
John Stough	25	13	56	23.2	12	14	85.7	23	38	1.52
Robert Henne	9	2	19	10.5	3	7	42.9	11	7	.78
Joe Hall	3	0	-	0	0	2	0	0	0	0

The team results for the 32-2 UK team of 1948-49

Date	Game	Result	Score	Notes
11/29/1948	Indiana Central at Kentucky	W	74 - 38	-
12/8/1948	Kentucky vs. DePaul	W	67 - 36	(at Louisville, KY)
12/10/1948	Tulsa at Kentucky	W	81 - 27	-
12/13/1948	Arkansas at Kentucky	W	76 - 39	-
12/16/1948	Kentucky at Holy Cross	W	51 - 48	(at Boston, MA)
12/18/1948	Kentucky vs. St. Johns	W	57 - 30	-
12/22/1948	Kentucky vs. Tulane	W	51 - 47	(at Louisville, KY)
12/29/1948	Kentucky vs. Tulane	W	78 - 47	Sugar Bowl (at New Orleans, LA)
12/30/1948	Kentucky vs. St. Louis	L	40 - 42	Sugar Bowl Championship (at New Orleans, LA)
1/11/1949	Kentucky vs. Bowling Green	W	63 - 61	(at Cleveland, OH)
1/15/1949	Kentucky at Tennessee	W	66 - 51	-
1/17/1949	Kentucky at Georgia Tech	W	56 - 45	-
1/22/1949	(#2) Kentucky at DePaul	W	56 - 45	-
1/29/1949	(#2) Kentucky vs. Notre Dame	W	62 - 38	(at Louisville, KY)
1/31/1949	(#2) Kentucky at Vanderbilt	W	72 - 50	-
2/2/1949	(#1) Kentucky at Alabama	W	56 - 40	-
2/3/1949	(#1) Kentucky vs. Mississippi	W	75 - 45	(at Memphis, TN)

Date	Matchup	W/L	Score	Notes
2/5/1949	(#1) Kentucky vs. (#18) Bradley	W	62 - 52	(at Owensboro, KY)
2/8/1949	Tennessee at (#1) Kentucky	W	71 - 56	-
2/12/1949	Xavier at (#1) Kentucky	W	96 - 50	-
2/14/1949	Alabama at (#1) Kentucky	W	74 - 32	-
2/16/1949	Mississippi at (#1) Kentucky	W	85 - 31	-
2/19/1949	Georgia Tech at (#1) Kentucky	W	78 - 32	-
2/21/1949	Georgia at (#1) Kentucky	W	95 - 40	-
2/24/1949	(#1) Kentucky at Xavier	W	51 - 40	-
2/26/1949	Vanderbilt at (#1) Kentucky	W	70 - 37	-
3/3/1949	(#1) Kentucky vs. Florida	W	73 - 36	SEC Tournament (at Louisville, KY)
3/4/1949	(#1) Kentucky vs. Auburn	W	70 - 39	SEC Tournament (at Louisville, KY)
3/5/1949	(#1) Kentucky vs. Tennessee	W	83 - 44	SEC Tournament (at Louisville, KY)
3/5/1949	(#1) Kentucky vs. (#7) Tulane	W	68 - 52	SEC Tournament Championship (at Louisville, KY)
3/14/1949	(#1) Kentucky vs. (#16) Loyola (Chicago)	L	56 - 67	NIT (at New York, NY)
3/21/1949	(#1) Kentucky vs. (#14) Villanova	W	85 - 72	NCAA Eastern Regional First Round (at New York, NY)
3/22/1949	(#1) Kentucky vs. (#4) Illinois	W	76 - 47	NCAA Eastern Regional Finals (at New York, NY)
3/26/1949	(#1) Kentucky vs. (#2) Oklahoma A&M	W	46 - 36	NCAA Championship (at Seattle, WA)

The UK-led U. S. basketball team
sailing for Europe in 1948

CHAPTER 6:

Fabulous Five Gone: 'Poor' Season Awaits

After two straight NCAA championships Coach Rupp faced a rebuilding year in 1949-50. Gone were Groza, Jones and Beard – the heart of the great teams of 1947-48-49.

The Fabulous Five was now history.

But Rupp did have one big weapon to use in 1949-50: Bill Spivey, Kentucky's first seven-foot center.

Rupp got the services of Spivey almost by default, just as he got his great guard Bobby Watson after he was turned down for scholarships at schools such as Alabama and Vanderbilt.

"When we first looked at Spivey we, too, were not interested in giving him a scholarship," said Rupp. "He was big, but he was as scrawny as he could be. But he came by to see me and ask for a chance to play on our team. I told him I couldn't use him. He stopped at every school in the Southeastern Conference. I think he weighed about 165 pounds. And, he came in and he begged, and he begged, he wanted to come to Kentucky. And I said, 'There's only one thing that you can do to play basketball; you've got to get your weight up to 200 pounds.' Harry and I arranged to get him a job down at William's Drug Store. Owen Williams was running a drugstore at the time, and he made him drink a lot of malted milks, and he fed him good, and during the time that I was over at the Olympics, I was getting wires and letters from Coach Lancaster. He said, 'Spivey now weighs 175 . . . he now weighs 183 . . . now weighs 193 . . . now weighs 200 pounds.' So I cabled him back collect, and said, 'I am convinced he can eat, but can he play?' Well, that was for us to find out later. And we found out later that he also could play. He certainly could play."

But Spivey was not enough.

In one 10-day period in January 1950 Kentucky lost three of five games after rising to as high as No. 2 in the nation in the ratings.

Rupp's team did win the Sugar Bowl tournament and the Southeastern Conference tournament, but their final regular season record of 25-4 did not earn them a chance to defend their NCAA title.

They even lost to Tennessee (56-43) for the first time in years as Wah Wah Jones little brother, Hugh, was a big factor for the Vols.

The Cats avenged that loss with a 95-58 win over Tennessee in the finals of the SEC tournament at Louisville in March of 1950.

The Wildcats returned to the NIT in New York and suffered Rupp's most embarrassing loss ever in the first round, getting drubbed 89-50 by unheralded City College of New York (CCNY).

Here is a report on that game by Louis Effrat in the New York Times:

C.C.N.Y. Trounces Kentucky, 89-50

NEW YORK, March 14, 1950 -- More vividly and eloquently than words, the figures tell the story of the worst defeat ever pinned on any Wildcat basketball team since the court sport was introduced at the Lexington university back in 1903. It happened last night at Madison Square Garden, where 18,000 fans saw Nat Holman's busy Beavers rout the second-seeded team, 89-50, in a quarter-final encounter in the thirteenth annual National Invitation Tournament.

Following another upset, in which Duquesne conquered La Salle, 49-47, the City College victory qualified the Lavender to oppose the Pittsburgh Dukes in one of tomorrow night's semi-fnals. St. John's will engage top-seeded Bradley in the other.

The City College-Kentucky clash pitted two of the nation's recognized master strategists, Nat Holman and Adolph Rupp, against each other in a battle of wits, which failed to materialize, for the C.C.N.Y. players, with a furious first half, gave neither celebrated coach time for thinking.

The Beavers turned the trick with baskets, some of them so spectacularly made that they left everyone, including Holman, breathless. On the other hand, Rupp, who had been named "Coach of the Year" by the Metropolitan Basketball Writers Association, would have had to be a magician to save the night.

Never in all his glorious twenty years as head man at Kentucky had a team tutored by Rupp been so humiliated. Run into the boards by the speedy Beavers, the Wildcats were virtually beaten in the first four and a half minutes. At this stage, C.C.N.Y. enjoyed a 13-1 spread, as Ed Warner, Ed Roman and Floyd Layne -- the first with his amazing shooting and feeding accuracy, the second with his flawless defense against the 7-foot Bill Spivey, and the third with his incredibly successful handling of rebounds -- completely dominated the struggle.

The Kentucky players were not permitted to catch their breaths. Seldom were they allotted too much room to get off their shots and except for one short span in the second half -- when they had cut a 26-point deficit to 16 -- as Spivey belatedly found the range, were made to look pitifully weak.

City College was great. None will question the superb play of the Beavers, who after they had dropped to a mere 54-38 advantage, clicked for sixteen straight points in slightly more than three minutes. Warner, Irwin, Dambrot, Roman, Layne -- every man in a City College uniform, in fact -- carried out his part sensationally. All this against a squad that Uncle Adolph had proclaimed "potentially the greatest team I ever have had."

When the Beavers needed to fast break, they did. When the set-up called a slowdown, they did. And when a pass or a rebound was required, they were there, on time and at the correct spot. Against such magnificence, there was little the Wildcats could do. Spivey, charged with four fouls in the first half, had to proceed with caution, and Jim Line, Walt Hirsch, Bobby Watson and Dale Barnstable were just "names" in so far as the victors were concerned.

Long before halftime, when C.C.N.Y., the Metropolitan ruler, but unseeded in this tourney, had a 45-20 lead, the Beavers had this one solidly sealed. Warner, feinting and curling in lay-ups from all angles, was the big gun, with a 26-point output. Roman netted 20 and still had time to excel on defense. Spivey's 15 was tops for the losers.

The night was full of surprises, including Holman's decision to start Watkins, who never before had done so at the Garden. However, Holman had Roman poised at the scorer's table and first-string center replaced him a few seconds after the opening tap. Watkins, a comparative unknown, was employed from time to time thereafter and like all the other Beavers, fared handsomely.

Kentucky 50

Player	FG	FGA	FT	FTA	PF	Ast	Pts
Jim Line	2	7	1	2	2	0	5
Shelby Linville	5	20	3	4	3	2	13
Walter Hirsch	1	12	0	0	1	3	2
Read Morgan	0	1	0	0	0	0	0
Bill Spivey	4	18	7	10	5	0	15
Bobby Watson	1	5	0	0	1	1	2
Leonard Pearson	3	6	1	1	5	2	7
Garland Townes	0	1	0	0	0	0	0
Dale Barnstable	3	11	0	0	3	2	6
Lucian Whitaker	0	1	0	0	1	0	0
Totals	**19**	**82**	**12**	**17**	**21**	**10**	**50**

CCNY - 89 (Head Coach: Nat Holman)

Player	FG	FGA	FT	FTA	PF	Ast	Pts
Irwin Dambrot	9	16	2	2	2	2	20
Ed Warner	10	18	6	11	3	5	26
Leroy Watkins	1	3	0	1	2	0	2
Ed Roman	8	18	1	1	5	0	17
Norm Mager	2	4	2	2	2	3	6
Alvin Roth	3	11	3	4	1	5	9
Herb Cohen	0	4	1	1	0	1	1
Mike Witlin	0	0	1	1	0	1	1
Arnold Smith	0	0	0	0	0	0	0
Floyd Layne	1	4	1	1	1	2	3
Ron Nadell	2	2	0	0	0	1	4
Artie Glass	0	0	0	0	0	0	0
Totals	**36**	**80**	**17**	**24**	**16**	**20**	**89**

The specter of point-shaving again reared its ugly head during the 1949-50 post season.

Englisis told officials Barnstable, Walter Hirsch and Jim Line were all involved in shaving points during the 1949-50 season. Englisis claimed the three conspired with him and his associates, including boss Eli Kaye, to shave points in a game against DePaul and a few weeks later against Arkansas. None of the players were ever convicted of shaving points on these allegations, however.

CHAPTER 7:

Wildcats Again Champs, But Storm Clouds Loom

Kentucky fans muted their unhappiness over their team's downfall of 1949-50 by seeing Coach Rupp field another super team for the 1950-51 season.

The Wildcats – led by Spivey, Cliff Hagan, Frank Ramsey and Lucian Whittaker -- roared to a 32-2 season, including a 97-61 win over Loyola of Chicago, erasing the memory of the point-shaving loss of two years earlier.

The Wildcats were upset 61-57 by Vanderbilt in the finals of the SEC tournament, but went into the NCAA tournament ranked No. 1 in the nation.

Rupp's boys upheld the ratings, roaring to their third NCAA championship in four years.

They knocked off Louisville 79-68 in the first round at Raleigh, beat St. Johns 59-43 in the East

Regional semifinals at New York City then beat Illinois 76-74 in the regional finals at New York. They then took out Kansas State 68-58 in the title game. Here is a report of the championship game:

MINNEAPOLIS (AP)- Ever start your car up a long hill only to have it stop halfway to the top because it ran out of gas?

That's also a description of Lew Hitch, Kansas State center, Tuesday night in the NCAA title-deciding game which Kentucky won, 68 to 58 with a rousing last half rally.

For the first half, Hitch, 6-foot-7 inch center, made 7-foot Bill Spivey, his Kentucky rival, look almost inexperienced.

Then came the second half.

Spivey kept right on going, Hitch all but stopped. And when Spivey took command of the rebounding, Kentucky wiped out a two-point half-time deficit to saunter to its third NCAA title in four years.

Hitch snagged nine rebounds during the entire game but only one came in the second half. Spivey split his 21 rebounds almost down the middle with 12 coming after the intermission, which found Kansas State ahead 29 to 27.

The big fellow's efforts brought a successful close to the second year of Coach Adolph Rupp's current three-year plan. He started almost from scratch some 17 months ago with a band of sophomores and incidental upper classmen. His aim was to win the 1952 NCAA crown and a possible trip to the 1952 Olympics.

But he has the big title a year early. Nine of the ten men on the squad return next season. Only exception is Roger Layne, third string center.

After the title conquest, Rupp gave most of the praise to Spivey's amazing second half effort but he also singled out Cliff Hagan for bouquets. Hagan, who missed the final practices because of flu, entered the game when it was almost 15 minutes old and with Kansas State ahead. Within minutes the score was tied only to have Kansas State edge ahead again and remain two points ahead at the recess.

After the intermission, Shelby Linville potted a free throw and then Spivey tipped in a two pointer to put Kentucky ahead. The blue grass Wildcats never again trailed.

Midway through the last half, with Spivey a demon under the baskets, the Kansans went eight full minutes without scoring. That, combined with Spivey, meant the ball game.

In addition to his defensive work, Spivey was the game's leading scorer with 22 points. That lifted his total to 72 for the four NCAA tourney games.

While the big center was getting the praises of his coach and the congratulations of his teammates, Coach Jack Gardner of the losing team thought some of the Kentucky credit should go to Bobby Watson, stubby guard.

"He is faster than Ralph Beard, guard on the Olympic team," moaned Gardner.

Spivey was the game's leading scorer with 22 points. That lifted his total to 72 for four NCAA tourney games.

Kentucky, replacing City College of New York in the NCAA top spot, was rated the No. 1 team in the Associated Press basketball poll.

In a foul-marked consolation game, Illinois defeated Oklahoma A & M, 61 to 46. Fifty personals were fouls were called, 31 on the Aggies.

After the NCAA tournament Kentucky was asked to play a series of exhibition games against Puerto Rican teams. UK won them all.

The 1951 NCAA championship game box score

Kentucky *68*

Player	FG	FGA	FT	FTA	Reb	PF	Pts
Lucian Whitaker	4	5	1	1	2	2	9
Shelby Linville	2	7	4	8	8	5	8
Bill Spivey	9	29	4	6	21	2	22
Frank Ramsey	4	10	1	3	4	5	9
Bobby Watson	3	8	2	4	3	3	8
Cliff Hagan	5	6	0	2	4	5	10
Lou Tsioropoulos	1	4	0	0	3	1	2
C. M. Newton	0	0	0	0	0	0	0
Totals	28	69	12	24	45	23	68

Kansas State *58*

Player	FG	FGA	FT	FTA	Reb	PF	Pts
Ed Head	3	11	2	2	3	2	8
Jack Stone	3	8	6	8	6	2	12
Lew Hitch	6	15	1	1	9	3	13
Ernie Barrett	2	12	0	2	3	1	4
Jim Iverson	3	12	1	2	0	3	7
Bob Rousey	2	10	0	0	2	3	4
John Gibson	0	2	1	1	1	5	1
Don Upson	0	1	0	0	2	1	0
Dick Knostman	1	4	1	2	3	1	3
Dick Peck	2	3	0	1	0	0	4
Dan Schuyler	1	2	0	1	1	2	2
Totals	23	80	12	20	30	23	58

The 1950-51 Kentucky player statistics

Player	Games Played	FG	FGA	%	FT	FTA	%	Total Rebs	F	Total Pts	PPG
Bill Spivey	33	252	632	39.9	131	211	62.1	567	91	635	19.24
Shelby Linville	34	151	388	38.9	53	70	75.7	309	91	355	10.44
Bobby Watson	34	151	460	32.8	51	68	75	86	78	353	10.38
Frank Ramsey	34	135	413	32.7	75	123	61	434	114	345	10.15
Cliff Hagan	20	69	188	36.7	45	61	73.8	169	62	183	9.15
Walter Hirsch	30	113	396	28.5	48	68	70.6	239	79	274	9.13
Lucian Whitaker	31	64	187	34.2	33	55	60	61	52	161	5.19
Lou Tsioropoulos	27	38	122	31.1	16	30	53.3	130	33	92	3.41
Read Morgan	17	19	-	?	6	11	54.5	-	19	44	2.59
Dwight Price	20	13	47	27.7	8	18	44.4	43	15	34	1.7
Roger Layne	12	6	-	?	7	11	63.6	-	14	19	1.58
C. M. Newton	18	8	35	22.9	7	11	63.6	13	13	23	1.28
Guy Strong	10	5	23	21.7	0	1	0	4	5	10	1
Paul Lansaw	12	4	-	?	3	4	75	-	9	11	.92
Lindle Castle	5	1	-	?	1	2	50	-	4	3	.6

The 1950-51 NCAA season game by game results:

Date	Game	Result	Score	Notes
12/1/1950	West Texas State at Kentucky	W	73 - 43	-
12/9/1950	Purdue at Kentucky	W	70 - 52	Memorial Coliseum Dedication
12/12/1950	Kentucky at Xavier	W	67 - 56	-
12/14/1950	Florida at Kentucky	W	85 - 37	-
12/16/1950	Kansas at Kentucky	W	68 - 39	-
12/23/1950	(#1) Kentucky vs. (#13) St. Johns	W	43 - 37	-
12/29/1950	(#1) Kentucky vs. St. Louis	L	42 - 43 OT	Sugar Bowl (at New Orleans, LA)
12/30/1950	(#1) Kentucky vs. Syracuse	W	69 - 59	Sugar Bowl (at New Orleans, LA)
1/5/1951	Auburn at (#3) Kentucky	W	79 - 35	-
1/8/1951	DePaul at (#3) Kentucky	W	63 - 55	-
1/13/1951	Alabama at (#3) Kentucky	W	65 - 48	-
1/15/1951	Notre Dame at (#3) Kentucky	W	69 - 44	-
1/20/1951	(#2) Kentucky at Tennessee	W	70 - 45	-
1/22/1951	(#2) Kentucky at Georgia Tech	W	82 - 61	-
1/27/1951	(#1) Kentucky at Vanderbilt	W	74 - 49	-
1/29/1951	(#1) Kentucky at Tulane	W	104 - 68	-

Date	Matchup	W/L	Score	Notes
1/31/1951	(#1) Kentucky at Louisiana State	W	81 - 59	-
2/2/1951	(#1) Kentucky at Mississippi State	W	80 - 60	-
2/3/1951	(#1) Kentucky vs. Mississippi	W	86 - 39	(at Owensboro, KY)
2/9/1951	Georgia Tech at (#1) Kentucky	W	75 - 42	-
2/13/1951	Xavier at (#1) Kentucky	W	78 - 51	-
2/17/1951	Tennessee at (#1) Kentucky	W	86 - 61	-
2/19/1951	(#1) Kentucky at DePaul	W	60 - 57	-
2/23/1951	Georgia at (#1) Kentucky	W	88 - 41	-
2/24/1951	Vanderbilt at (#1) Kentucky	W	89 - 57	-
3/1/1951	(#1) Kentucky vs. Mississippi State	W	92 - 70	SEC Tournament (at Louisville, KY)
3/2/1951	(#1) Kentucky vs. Auburn	W	84 - 54	SEC Tournament (at Louisville, KY)
3/3/1951	(#1) Kentucky vs. Georgia Tech	W	82 - 56	SEC Tournament (at Louisville, KY)
3/3/1951	(#1) Kentucky vs. Vanderbilt	L	57 - 61	SEC Tournament Championship (at Louisville, KY)
3/13/1951	Loyola (Chicago) at (#1) Kentucky	W	97 - 61	-
3/20/1951	(#1) Kentucky vs. Louisville	W	79 - 68	NCAA East Regional First Round (at Raleigh, NC)
3/22/1951	(#1) Kentucky vs. (#9) St. Johns	W	59 - 43	NCAA East Regional Semifinals (at New York, NY)
3/24/1951	(#1) Kentucky vs. (#5) Illinois	W	76 - 74	NCAA East Regional Finals (at New York, NY)
3/27/1951	(#1) Kentucky vs. (#4) Kansas State	W	68 - 58	NCAA Championship (at Minneapolis, MN)

Date	Opponent	Result	Score	Notes
4/27/1951	Kentucky All-Stars at Kentucky	W	94 - 49	Exhibition
8/25/1951	Kentucky at San German Athletic Club	W	86 - 38	Exhibition (at Puerto Rico)
8/26/1951	Kentucky at Ponce Lions	W	83 - 43	Exhibition (at Puerto Rico)
8/27/1951	Kentucky at San Turce	W	93 - 40	Exhibition (at Puerto Rico)
8/29/1951	Kentucky at University Puerto Rico	W	91 - 44	Exhibition (at Puerto Rico)
9/2/1951	Kentucky vs. Navy	W	52 - 23	Exhibition (at Puerto Rico) [Called at half due to rain.]
9/3/1951	Kentucky at University Puerto Rico	W	75 - 46	Exhibition (at Puerto Rico)

CHAPTER 8:

Point-Shaving Scandal in Full Bloom

Big Blue fans were in seventh heaven at this point, the Wildcats having won the national championship three of the last four years and the legendary Fabulous Five making headlines in the NBA.

The ex-Wildcats had been offered some great financial deals by a group of business men – forming their own professional team, called the Indianapolis Olympians.

The former UK players felt they had managed to escape their point-shaving problems and were having a great season in the pros, Beard and Groza ranking among the top 10 players in the league.

The 1951-52 team was following in the footsteps of the 1950-51 champions as they rolled to a 29-3 record and advanced to the finals of the Eastern Regional before the No.1-rated Wildcats were upset by St. Johns 64-57 at Raleigh.

The UK results for 1951-52

Date	Game	Result	Score	Notes
12/8/1951	Washington & Lee at Kentucky	W	96 - 46	-
12/10/1951	Kentucky at Xavier	W	97 - 72	-
12/13/1951	(#1) Kentucky at Minnesota	L	57 - 61	-
12/17/1951	(#2) St. Johns at (#1) Kentucky	W	81 - 40	-
12/20/1951	DePaul at (#2) Kentucky	W	98 - 60	-
12/26/1951	UCLA at (#1) Kentucky	W	84 - 53	-
12/28/1951	(#1) Kentucky vs. Brigham Young	W	84 - 64	Sugar Bowl (at New Orleans, LA)
12/29/1951	(#1) Kentucky vs. (#12) St. Louis	L	60 - 61	Sugar Bowl Championship (at New Orleans, LA)
1/3/1952	(#4) Kentucky vs. Mississippi	W	116 - 58	(at Owensboro, KY)
1/5/1952	Louisiana State at (#4) Kentucky	W	57 - 47	-
1/7/1952	Xavier at (#4) Kentucky	W	83 - 50	-
1/12/1952	(#3) Kentucky at Florida	W	99 - 52	-
1/14/1952	(#3) Kentucky vs. Georgia	W	95 - 55	(at Louisville, KY)
1/19/1952	(#3) Kentucky at Tennessee	W	65 - 56	-
1/21/1952	(#3) Kentucky at Georgia Tech	W	96 - 51	-
1/26/1952	(#3) Kentucky at Alabama	W	71 - 67	-

Date	Opponent	W/L	Score	Notes
1/28/1952	(#3) Kentucky at Vanderbilt	W	88 - 51	-
1/30/1952	(#1) Kentucky at Auburn	W	88 - 48	-
2/2/1952	(#1) Kentucky vs. Notre Dame	W	71 - 66	(at Chicago, IL)
2/4/1952	Tulane at (#1) Kentucky	W	103 - 54	-
2/6/1952	Mississippi at (#1) Kentucky	W	81 - 61	-
2/9/1952	Georgia Tech at (#1) Kentucky	W	93 - 42	-
2/11/1952	Mississippi State at (#1) Kentucky	W	110 - 66	-
2/16/1952	Tennessee at (#1) Kentucky	W	95 - 40	-
2/21/1952	Vanderbilt at (#1) Kentucky	W	75 - 45	-
2/23/1952	(#1) Kentucky at DePaul	W	63 - 61	-
2/28/1952	(#1) Kentucky vs. Georgia Tech	W	80 - 59	SEC Tournament (at Louisville, KY)
2/29/1952	(#1) Kentucky vs. Tulane	W	85 - 61	SEC Tournament (at Louisville, KY)
3/1/1952	(#1) Kentucky vs. Tennessee	W	81 - 66	SEC Tournament (at Louisville, KY)
3/1/1952	(#1) Kentucky vs. Louisiana State	W	44 - 43	SEC Tournament Championship (at Louisville, KY)
3/21/1952	(#1) Kentucky vs. Penn State	W	82 - 54	NCAA East Regional First Round (at Raleigh, NC)
3/22/1952	(#1) Kentucky vs. (#10) St. Johns	L	57 - 64	NCAA East Regional Finals (at Raleigh, NC)

UK 57

Player	FG	FT	Pts
Lou Tsioropoulos	0	0	0
Lucian Whitaker	3	3	9
Shelby Linville	1	2	4
Willie Rouse	0	0	0
Cliff Hagan	9	4	22
Gayle Rose	1	0	2
Bobby Watson	1	2	4
Frank Ramsey	5	4	14
Billy Evans	1	0	2
Totals	21	15	57

St. Johns - *64 (Head Coach: Frank McGuire)*

Player	FG	FT	Pts
Jack McMahon	8	2	18
Jim Davis	1	0	2
Jim Walsh	1	2	4
Bob Zawoluk	12	8	32
Ronnie MacGilvray	1	3	5

Dick Duckett	1	1	3
Solly Walker	0	0	0
Totals	24	16	64

The Wildcats had plenty of stars returning for 1952-53 and were the preseason choice to win it all once again.

But then the bottom fell out as the point-shaving scandals became the nation's top sports story as a result of investigations by New York City officials.

The whole thing started when Junius Kellogg, a star of the Manhattan Jaspers basketball squad, was offered $1,000 to throw a game. He told school officials about it and they contacted the New York District Attorney's office. The floodgates opened when Manhattan District Attorney Frank Hogan conducted an investigation which implicated 33 players in 86 games. And those were just the ones they knew about.

Because the offenses happened in New York City, Hogan had jurisdiction to hand down indictments.

Manhattan College, Long Island University, New York University and CCNY were among the early schools hit by the investigations. The stories made the front page of the New York Times.

CCNY and LIU were the first national caliber teams hit, with Hogan ordering the arrest of several players, including all-American Sherman White of LIU on Feb. 18, 1951. White was the college player of the year and led the nation in scoring at 27.7 points per game.

White admitted receiving $5,500 from gamblers to shave points and actually throw games. He had several teammates who also admitted taking part in the point-shaving and deliberate loss of games.

White told Hogan: "After the N.C. State game, (teammate) Eddie Gard befriended me. We sat down and started talking. He brought in (teammates) Bigos and Fuertado. He gave me the same old story: 'We control the game. We're good enough to beat these guys anyway and we can make some money. They ain't giving you no money here at L.I.U.' The same old story. We can control the game and nobody will get hurt except the gamblers. Now I'm one of the guys. Peer pressure."

When the stories broke about the basketball fixing scandals in New York City, sports writers asked Coach Rupp if he thought any Kentucky players might eventually be involved.

"Those gamblers couldn't touch my boys with a 10-foot pole," he told writers.

Privately, Rupp met with his assistant coach, Harry Lancaster at Rupp's farm, where he raised purebred cattle, to talk about the situation.

"Harry, this New York stuff is pretty damn horrible," Rupp told Lancaster. "I told the writers there is no way our boys would have done anything like that. I never saw any evidence or indications some of them might be trying to affect the score, did you?"

"The only games I think there is even any possibility of that having happened was the Loyola and CCNY games," said Lancaster. "Times are tough and I could see how gamblers could buy a few players for a few thousand dollars. Especially, some of those boys who had tough home situations."

A 1940s hollow warning

IMPORTANT NOTICE
BETTING OR SOLICITING BETS
IS PROHIBITED
IN MADISON SQUARE GARDEN
Spectators must occupy the seats their tickets call for and must not leave them before or during any event unless it is absolutely necessary to do so. Spectators at all events must comport themselves in such a manner as not to disturb or offend other spectators.
Violators of the above rules will be removed from Madison Square Garden and will not be allowed admittance to any subsequent events.
Madison Square Garden Corporation

It would not be long before Kentucky got caught up in the scandal.

On Oct. 20, 1951, Hogan ordered the arrest of Beard, Groza and Barnstable for accepting bribes to shave points in their NIT game against Loyola of Chicago in Madison Square Garden in 1949.

Beard's worst fears had come back to haunt him.

The Wildcats all confessed to taking money to control the score of the Loyola game.

"We took some money, but we never ever did anything to cause us to lose a game," Beard said later. "I would rather have died first."

Manhattan General Sessions Court Judge Saul Streit in May 1952 handed out suspended sentences to Groza, Beard and Barnstable on their guilty plea to a lesser charge of conspiracy (rather than the more serious charge of taking a bribe) and placed them on indefinite probation and barred them from all sports for three years. NBA commissioner Maurice Podoloff also suspended the trio and the Indianapolis Olympians pro team folded.

Judge Streit presided over the entire cases involving all of the schools. He was especially tough on the ex-LIU star White, handing him a 12-month sentence to serve in Rikers Island, the main prison in New York City. White served 8 months and 24 days). Additionally, he and all of the other players involved in the scandal were banned from ever playing in the NBA.

Judge Streit had the duty of sentencing 14 players. All had pleaded guilty. Judge Streit listened gravely to the recommendations of the district attorney, who wanted all the boys left unpunished as an encouragement to others to testify against the gamblers.

But Streit would have none of it. He sentenced five players to prison for six months to three years. He freed nine on probation, including the UK players.

Later, Kentucky's All-American center, Bill Spivey, was also suspected of being involved in point-shaving and (at the school's suggestion) took himself out of the lineup in 1952 while he tried to clear his name. He had averaged 19.24 points a game for the 1950-51 team. He never played another game for the Wildcats.

As it turned out, the investigation dragged on through the entire 1951–52 season.

Two teammates allegedly claimed to school officials that Spivey was actively involved in the point-shaving scheme. Spivey denied any involvement, admitting only to not telling anyone about being approached by a gambler who wanted him to shave points. He denied ever taking any money or shaving points. School officials, however, weren't convinced, and expelled Spivey from school in March 1952.

On June 9, 1952 Spivey was arrested in New York, and was released pending a trial, which started in January 1953.

Spivey's former teammate, Walter Hirsch, testified that Spivey asked to be included as a point shaver, and was upset that the payment for his role in shaving during the 1950 Sugar Bowl game was less than he was expecting.

But Hirsch's testimony differed greatly from his earlier grand jury testimony, which had no mention of Spivey's involvement.

Hirsch also told the grand jury that Spivey and gambler Jack West, the ringleader, had not met. West declined to testify, leading to criminal contempt charges against him.

Spivey again denied taking part in the scandal, saying he had turned down a different gambler on two occasions. The trial lasted for 13 days before the case went to a jury.

By a 9–3 margin, the majority of jurors supported acquittal for Spivey, and the hung jury caused a mistrial. The grand jury eventually dropped the charges against Spivey.

Though vindicated in the courts, Spivey was never able to take advantage of his fantastic hoops skills in the professional ranks.

NBA Commissioner Maurice Podoloff banned him from signing with any of the league's teams. Claiming that he had been blacklisted, Spivey filed a lawsuit against the NBA and Podoloff in 1960, seeking more than $800,000 in damages. He eventually settled out of court for $10,000 after his lawyers told him the case could linger on for years.

Former Kentucky coach Joe B. Hall said, "Most people feel he would have been one of the top five centers of all-time had he had the chance to mature in the NBA."

Banished from the NBA, Spivey spent his professional career playing for numerous minor league and barnstorming teams.

The SEC had voted to suspend Kentucky from conference play for the 1952-53 season so UK athletic director Bernie Shively had lined up more than a dozen games against non-conference teams. But they would not get to play any of them.

Perhaps being overzealous, the NCAA, claiming additional violations had occurred, including Rupp breaking rules by giving players money, handed Kentucky basketball what was in effect the "death penalty" in 1952, telling member schools not to schedule the Wildcats for the 1952-53 season. This, in reality, killed the entire season.

The exact charges against Kentucky by the NCAA included:

1. In the spring of 1948 members of the basketball team on their departure for the NCAA tournament were given $50 each by sports enthusiasts not connected with the university.
2. In the spring of 1949 before their departure for the NCAA tournament members of the basketball team were given $50 each by sports enthusiasts not connected with the university.
3. Before the Kentucky team left for the St. John's game in New York City in December, 1950, six of the players were given $50 each.

4. After the basketball team returned from the Sugar Bowl game in January, 1951, several of the players were given sums ranging from $25 to $50 by coaches.
5. Between October, 1946, and December, 1950, two members of the basketball team had received monthly stipends of $50 from sports enthusiasts not connected with the university.

"I have no doubt in my mind that we would have won the NCAA championship in 1952-53 had we been allowed to play," said Rupp.

CHAPTER 9:

Punishment Fallout Disastrous

The Kentucky players came clean when talking with investigators, telling them the entire story of their involvement and their regrets for ever having become entangled with the gamblers.

"Those guys were smooth talkers. They should have been salesmen. They took us out for a stroll, treated us to a meal, and before we knew anything, we were right in the middle of it. They said we didn't have to dump the game. They said nobody would get hurt except other gamblers. They said everybody was doing it. And they asked what was wrong with winning a game by as many points as we could. We just didn't think. But if somebody suspected what was going on at the Garden had warned us that things like that were against the law, we'd never have done it," Dale Barnstable told author Charlie Rosen.

The Kentucky players were fully cooperative with the investigation, as evidenced by a statement by New York Assistant District Attorney Vincent O'Connor to the court that was sitting in judgment of the players. O'Conner's statement as printed in the Lexington Herald on April 30, 1952:

"With respect to the defendants before the court for sentence, I do know that they have previously given your honor information concerning the details of their involvement and their personal family and environmental background.

"On behalf of the District Atty. Hogan I am going to ask for clemency for these defendants.

"I first met Groza and Beard last October in Chicago in the office of the Cook county prosecutor, the Hon. John S. Boyle, who has co-operated splendidly in several phases of our investigation. At the same time my associate, Asst. Dist. Atty. William P. Sirignano, was in Louisville, questioning Barnstable.

"These three young men must have felt their world crashing in on them when approached by the police for questioning. Groza and Beard were, at that time, part owners and stars of a leading professional basketball team, the Indianapolis Olympians. Barnstable was a highly-regarded Louisville teacher and athletic coach.

"Our appeal to these young men was that which had secured the facts from every player questioned throughout the entire basketball fix inquiry with the single exception of the misguided and ill-advised Spivey.

"It was: That the players owed it to themselves, to their families, to their universities, to society and to the sport itself to help us clean out widespread corruption which threatened basketball's very existence. If that meant involving themselves, it was only because the truth called for such involvement.

"We told them to place confidence in us to be fair to them if they were of assistance to our inquiry.

"When Groza and Beard had responded and given me the facts I asked Groza to speak over the telephone to Louisville to Barnstable and encourage him to be frank and open.

"None present, I am sure, will forget that tense moment in the Chicago prosecutor's office when Groza said over the long-distance telephone to Barnstable, 'Barney, Ralph and I have told these men the truth, and I think you should do the same. You'll feel all the better for it.'

"Barnstable quickly, then, did tell Mr. Sirignano the truth, for he, like Groza and Beard, and the many players from New York, Ohio, Illinois and Kentucky, were possessed of the stuff for rehabilitation and rebuilding worthwhile and useful lives.

"These three defendants became of substantial aid to our office. Groza and Beard waived extradition and came to

New York. Barnstable voluntarily accompanied a detective from Kentucky for arrest here. All three expressed desired to waive immunity and testify before the grand jury.

"They were content to trust our advice that while they faced prosecution it would be to their best interests to cooperate fully. It was only at our urging that they sought advice of counsel, the New York attorney appointed for them by the court.

"They were important witnesses in the grand jury. Testimony given by them has contributed substantially to the indictment of eight fixers, four of whom have already been convicted by guilty pleas entered in the face of overwhelming proof.

"The defendants are available as trial witnesses should it become necessary to call them to bring to justice the remainder of the fixers whose prosecutions are pending. We told these young men that at the appropriate time we would ask the court to consider their cooperation with our office in passing judgment on them. At the time of their formal admission of guilt the court accepted misdemeanor rather than felony pleas from them on our recommendation."

Judge Streit was not very knowledgeable about how college sports operated and based his rulings and opinions primarily on testimony by players and others.

He blasted college sports in general and was especially critical of Coach Rupp and Kentucky, distortedly claiming Rupp had actually endangered the health of his players and condoned rules violations.

Kentucky school and government officials came to Rupp's defense and, in effect, told Judge Streit to get lost, that they would manage their own athletic programs and try to keep teams within the rules prescribed by the SEC and NCAA.

Salvatore (Tori) Sollazzo of New York City, the original mastermind behind the basketball point-shaving scheme, served 12 years in prison and was handed a $1,128,493 bill for tax evasion.

The harsh punishment handed Kentucky by the SEC and NCAA drew a lot of criticism from the national media, which, in essence, said Kentucky was used as a rules scapegoat.

Some of their comments included:

Arch Ward of the <u>Chicago Tribune</u>, *"We make no defense of any university which professes to live up to the rules of the unit to which it belongs and then violates them willfully . . . But the NCAA council knows that its disclosures of the $25 and $50 gifts received by Kentucky basketball players, from outside the school or within, was peanuts. . . Many universities whose athletic prominence equals or excels Kentucky's would be placed on probation, as has Kentucky, if penalties were applied generally. . .Comparable violations occur in groups which supposedly are models of all* *that is good and holy in athletic administration . ."* Ed Danforth of the <u>Atlanta Journal</u> noted *"If every athlete in the nation who has been given such assistance by fans were disqualified, the boys would have a hard time fielding teams for the coming week end."*

Pat Harmon of the <u>Cincinnati Post</u> wrote: *"It's a laugh. Certainly Kentucky is guilty of permitting its athletes to accept side payments, but so is almost every other member of the NCAA. It's been going on for years. The writer has been present when cash payments were made to athletes at a Big Ten school."*

Tom Easterling, the sports editor of the UK student newspaper The Kentucky Kernel also accused SEC boss Bernie Moore of conniving to have Kentucky punished beyond SEC strictures. He claimed Moore, had assured UK Dean Ab Kirwan that he would go before the NCAA Council to urge them not to take additional action against Kentucky. But Easterling claimed, *"Moore, a member of the executive committee, was in Chicago at the same time the council was acting on the UK case, but he never made an appearance before the council, as he had promised to do."* Not only didn't Moore plead on behalf of Kentucky, but per Byers own memoirs it was Moore who was the driving force behind the NCAA's further actions against the school. Moore was in actuality secretly back-stabbing Kentucky while professing to be working in the school's best interest."

As with the SEC ruling and Judge Streit before him, while UK President Donovan did admit that wrongdoing had occurred, he did take issue with some of the particular findings and the overall harshness of the punishment. *"It is the opinion of our athletics board that the penalty inflicted upon the University of Kentucky is unduly severe and far more harsh than any penalty that has ever been inflicted upon a member for violation of the NCAA rules in the past."* wrote Donovan to NCAA President Hugh C. Willett.

As to allegations against Coach Rupp, UK President Donovan in 1952 declared: (Coach Rupp) *"did not knowingly violate the athletic rules or ethics. If I thought otherwise, I would have dismissed him."*

As to the money given to players after the Sugar Bowl appearances, Donovan said, *"I and other university officials knew about and approved the $50 given to basketball players, after two appearances in the Sugar Bowl. When we first appeared in football bowls we learned that it was customary among all schools going to bowls to give their players extraordinary expense money. When* *we went to the Orange Bowl, we asked the Southeastern Conference about the expense money and were told we could award each player $200. When we went to the Sugar bowl, we received permission to give the players $250. From that we reasoned it also would be within the rules to award basketball players $50 expense money after the Sugar Bowl basketball tournaments."*

Said Donovan about Rupp: *"Adolph Rupp is an arrogant man, given to sharp repartee and cutting sarcasm. He is awkward in public relations and a genius for saying the wrong thing. He also happens to be the best basketball coach in America. This last qualification also figured strongly in what later happened to us."* (Atlanta Journal and Constitution December 17, 1952.)

The cancellation of the 1952-53 season was not entirely bad for Kentucky.

Coach Rupp got many of his star players, such as Hagan and Ramsey, to delay their graduation a year so they could return in 1953-54 and he conducted long practice sessions working on plays and situations. He also conducted open scrimmage games, most attended by more than 10,000 fans.

A bitter Coach Rupp was looking to get revenge from NCAA President Walter Byers, vowing not to retire *" until the man who said Kentucky can't play in the NCAA hands me the national championship trophy."*

Rupp's 1954 team finished 25-0, but the NCAA ruled several graduate school students. Including Hagan and Ramsey, would not be eligible to play in the NCAA tournament. This, even though other graduate students had played in the NCAA tournament in the past. UK declined to take part in the tournament, but Rupp got his wish in 1958 with his last national championship with his famed Fiddlin' Five team.

Kentucky's 25-0 season of 1953-54

Date	Game	Result	Score	Notes
12/5/1953	Temple at Kentucky	W	86 - 59	-
12/12/1953	(#2) Kentucky at Xavier	W	81 - 66	-
12/14/1953	Wake Forest at (#2) Kentucky	W	101 - 69	-
12/18/1953	(#2) Kentucky at St. Louis	W	71 - 59	-
12/21/1953	(#13) Duke at (#2) Kentucky	W	85 - 69	UKIT
12/22/1953	(#20) LaSalle at (#2) Kentucky	W	73 - 60	UKIT Championship
12/28/1953	(#8) Minnesota at (#2) Kentucky	W	74 - 59	-
1/4/1954	Xavier at (#1) Kentucky	W	77 - 71	-
1/9/1954	Georgia Tech at (#1) Kentucky	W	105 - 53	-
1/11/1954	DePaul at (#1) Kentucky	W	81 - 63	-
1/16/1954	Tulane at (#1) Kentucky	W	94 - 43	-
1/23/1954	(#1) Kentucky at Tennessee	W	97 - 71	-
1/30/1954	(#1) Kentucky at Vanderbilt	W	85 - 63	-
2/2/1954	(#1) Kentucky vs. Georgia Tech	W	99 - 48	(at Louisville, KY)
2/4/1954	Georgia at (#1) Kentucky	W	106 - 55	-
2/6/1954	(#1) Kentucky vs. Georgia	W	100 - 68	(at Owensboro, KY)
2/8/1954	(#1) Kentucky at Florida	W	97 - 55	-
2/13/1954	Mississippi at (#1) Kentucky	W	88 - 62	-
2/15/1954	Mississippi State at (#1) Kentucky	W	81 - 49	-
2/18/1954	Tennessee at (#2)	W	90 - 63	-

		Kentucky			
2/20/1954		(#2) Kentucky at DePaul	W	76 - 61	-
2/22/1954		Vanderbilt at (#2) Kentucky	W	100 - 64	-
2/27/1954		(#2) Kentucky vs. Auburn	W	109 - 79	(at Montgomery, AL)
3/1/1954		(#2) Kentucky at Alabama	W	68 - 43	-
3/9/1954		(#1) Kentucky vs. (#7) Louisiana State	W	63 - 56	SEC Playoff (at Nashville, TN)

Kentucky player stats for 1953-54

Player	Games Played	FG	FGA	%	FT	FTA	%	Total Rebs	F	Total Pts	PPG
Cliff Hagan	25	234	514	45.5	132	191	69.1	338	80	600	24
Frank Ramsey	25	179	430	41.6	132	181	72.9	221	83	490	19.6
Lou Tsioropoulos	25	137	390	35.1	89	129	69	240	90	363	14.52
Billy Evans	25	86	231	37.2	49	63	77.8	180	65	221	8.84
Gayle Rose	23	56	162	34.6	42	65	64.6	31	67	154	6.7
Phil Grawemeyer	25	64	172	37.2	19	35	54.3	152	63	147	5.88
Linville Puckett	24	44	149	29.5	35	51	68.6	53	52	123	5.13
Jerry Bird	4	4	17	23.5	6	8	75	12	10	14	3.5
Bill Bibb	16	10	32	31.3	7	12	58.3	25	13	27	1.69
Hugh Coy	11	4	14	28.6	6	10	60	11	20	14	1.27
Willie Rouse	5	2	9	22.2	2	4	50	1	5	6	1.2
Dan Chandler	7	2	5	40	3	3	100	0	7	7	1
Jess Curry	9	2	17	11.8	4	8	50	4	8	8	.89
Harold Hurst	7	2	9	22.2	2	12	16.7	19	4	6	.86
Clay Evans	7	2	5	40	0	4	0	2	7	4	.57
Pete Grigsby	3	0	2	0	1	2	50	2	0	1	.33

A writer for Time Magazine in 1951 said the hoops scandals did open the eyes of many to the dangers of sports gambling and would serve as the catalyst to cleaning up college sports.

The scandals also put a horrible stain on a golden era of Kentucky basketball.

But the Wildcats basketball program continued to thrive and returned to the top of the national heap with NCAA championships in 1978, 1996 and 1998 and presently ranks among the nation's top teams as Coach John Calipari has made his team a regular NCAA championship contender and among the top five each season.

THE END

Kentucky's Fabulous Five of 1948

Ralph Beard

12

Hometown: Louisville, KY *(Male)*
Position: G **Playing Height:** 5-10 **Playing Weight:** 175
Date of Birth: December 2, 1927
Date of Death: November 29, 2007

Legal Name: Milton M. Beard

Kentucky Career Notes:
Olympic Champion
Retired Jersey #12
Multi-Sport Player [Football and Baseball]
Season Notes:
1945-46: All-SEC [First Team]; All-SEC Tournament
1946-47: All-American [Consensus (1st), NABC (1st), Converse (1st), True Magazine (1st), Helms (1st)]; All-SEC [First Team]; All-SEC Tournament
1947-48: All-American [Consensus (1st), AP (1st), NABC (1st), Converse (1st), True Magazine (1st), Helms (1st)]; All-SEC [First Team]; All-SEC Tournament
1948-49: All-American [Consensus (1st), AP (1st), UPI (1st), NABC (1st), Converse (2nd), Helms, Look (2nd), Sporting News (3rd), Colliers (1st)]; All-SEC [First Team (AP)]; All-SEC Tournament
Post-UK Career Notes:
Served in the Military
Drafted in the 2nd Round of the 1949 NBA Draft by Chicago
Professional Basketball Statistics *[External Link]*

Season	Games Played	FG	FT	FTA	%	F	Total Points
1945-46	30	111	57	110	51.8	69	279
1946-47	37	157	78	115	67.8	71	392
1947-48	38	194	88	149	59.1	80	476
1948-49	34	144	82	115	71.3	55	370
Total	**139**	*606*	*305*	*489*	*62.4*	*275*	**1517**

Alex Groza

15

Hometown: Martins Ferry, OH *(High)*
Position: C **Playing Height:** 6-7 **Playing Weight:** 220
Date of Birth: October 7, 1926
Date of Death: January 21, 1995

Career Notes:
Olympic Champion
Retired Jersey #15
Season Notes:
1944-45: (Drafted in Army part-way through season)
1946-47: All-American [Consensus (1st), NABC (1st), Converse (2nd), True Magazine (1st), Helms (2nd)]; All-SEC [Second Team]; All-SEC Tournament
1947-48: All-American [Consensus (2nd), AP (2nd), NABC (2nd), Converse (1st), True Magazine (2nd), Helms (2nd)]; NCAA Final Four Most Outstanding Player; NCAA Regional Most Outstanding Player; All-SEC

[First Team]; All-SEC Tournament

1948-49: National Player of the Year [Helms*]; All-American [Consensus (1st), AP (1st), UPI (1st), Converse (1st), Helms (1st), Look Magazine (1st), Sporting News (1st)]; NCAA Final Four Most Outstanding Player; NCAA Regional Most Outstanding Player; All-SEC [First Team (AP)]; All-SEC Tournament

Served in the Military
Drafted #2 Overall in the 1st Round of the 1949 NBA Draft by Indianapolis

Season	Games Played	FG	FT	FTA	%	F	Total Points
1944-45	10	62	41	57	71.9	-	165
1946-47	37	146	101	160	63.1	85	393
1947-48	39	200	88	140	62.9	87	488
1948-49	34	259	180	248	72.6	103	698
Total	**120**	*667*	*410*	*605*	*67.8*	*275*	**1744**

Wallace (Wah Wah) Jones

27

Hometown: Harlan, KY *(High)*
Position: F-C **Playing Height:** 6-4 **Playing Weight:** 205
Date of Birth: July 14, 1926
Kentucky Career Notes:
Olympic Champion
Retired Jersey #27
Multi-Sport Player [Football and Baseball]
Season Notes:
1945-46: All-SEC [First Team]; All-SEC Tournament
1946-47: All-American [Converse (2nd), Helms (2nd)]; All-SEC [First Team]; All-SEC Tournament
1947-48: All-American [Converse (3rd), True Magazine (3rd)]; All-SEC [First Team]; All-SEC Tournament
1948-49: All-American [Consensus (2nd), AP (2nd), UPI (1st), Converse (1st), Look (3rd), Sporting News (2nd)]; All-SEC [First Team (AP)]; All-SEC Tournament
Post-UK Career Notes:

Drafted #9 Overall in the 1st Round of the 1949 NBA Draft by Washington

Season	Games Played	FG	FT	FTA	%	F	Total Points
1945-46	30	105	80	126	63.5	83	290
1946-47	33	87	43	78	55.1	38	217
1947-48	36	133	69	103	67	82	335
1948-49	32	130	49	75	65.3	88	309
Total	127 *(-4)*	**455**	**241**	**382**	63.1	*291*	**1151**

Kenny Rollins

26

Hometown: Wickliffe, KY
Position: G **Playing Height:** 6-0 **Playing Weight:** 175
Date of Birth: July 14, 1923
Legal Name: Kenneth Herman Rollins
Olympic Champion Retired Jersey #26
Season Notes:
1946-47: All-SEC [First Team]; All-SEC Tournament
1947-48: All-SEC [First Team]; All-SEC Tournament
Post-UK Career Notes:
Served in the Military
Drafted in the 1948 NBA Draft by Fort Wayne

Season	Games Played
1942-43	22
1946-47	37
1947-48	39
Total	98

Cliff Barker

23

Hometown: Yorktown, IN *(High)*
Position: G-F **Playing Height:** 6-2 **Playing Weight:** 185
Date of Birth: January 15, 1921 *[Cumberland - 37 - 21]*
Date of Death: March 17, 1998
Legal Name: Clifford Eugene Barker
Kentucky Career Notes:
Olympic Champion
Retired Jersey #23
Season Notes:
1947-48: All-SEC [Second Team]; All-SEC Tournament
1948-49: All-SEC [Second Team (AP)]; All-SEC Tournament
Post-UK Career Notes:
Served in the Military
Drafted in the 1949 NBA Draft by Indianapolis

Season	Games Played	FG	FGA	%	FT	FTA	%	F	Total Points
1946-47	34	52	161	32.3	16	31	51.6	27	120
1947-48	38	98	317	30.9	52	93	55.9	101	248
1948-49	34	94	315	29.8	60	88	68.2	99	248
Total	106	244	793	30.8	128	212	60.4	227	616

Kentucky Coach Adolph Rupp

Overall Kentucky Record: 876 - 190
Years Coached: 1930-31 to 1971-72 (41 seasons)
Major Championships: 4 NCAA, 2 NIT, 1 Olympics
Date of Birth: September 2, 1901
Date of Death: December 10, 1977
Hometown: Halstead, KS
Alma Mater: Kansas [1923]

Sentences dispensed by Judge Streit

Name	Role	Punishment
Al Roth	CCNY player	sentenced to 6 months in a workhouse, but sentence was suspended when Streit approved Roth's decision to enter the Army.
Ed Warner	CCNY player	sentenced to 6 months in jail
Ed Roman	CCNY player	suspended sentence
Herb Cohen	CCNY player	suspended sentence
Irwin Dambrot	CCNY player	a dental school student at Columbia, he was given a suspended sentence
Norman Mager	CCNY player	suspended sentence
Floyd Lane	CCNY player	suspended sentence
Natie Miller	LIU player	suspended sentence
Lou Lipman	LIU player	suspended sentence
Adolph Bigos	LIU player	suspended sentence
Dick Feurtado	LIU player	suspended sentence
LeRoy Smith	LIU player	suspended sentence
Sherman White	LIU player	sentenced to one year in prison; served nine months on Rikers Island
Gene Melchiorre	Bradley player	suspended sentence
Bill Mann	Bradley player	suspended sentence
George Chianakos	Bradley player	suspended sentence
Bud Grover	Bradley player	acquitted
Aaron Preece	Bradley player	acquitted
Jim Kelly	Bradley player	acquitted
Fred Schlictman	Bradley player	acquitted
Connie Schaaf	NYU player	received a six month suspended sentence
Dale Barnstable	Kentucky player	suspended sentence
Ralph Beard	Kentucky player	suspended sentence
Alex Groza	Kentucky player	suspended sentence
Jack Byrnes	Manhattan player	placed on 3 years probation by Judge James M. Barrett
Henry Poppe	Manhattan player	placed on 3 years probation by Judge James M. Barrett
Bill Waller	Toledo player	charges dropped
Carlo Muzi	Toledo player	charges dropped
Bob McDonald	Toledo player	charges dropped
Jack Freeman	Toledo player	charges dropped
Salvatore Sollazzo	fixer	8 to 16 years in state prison

Eddie Gard	agent/former LIU player	indeterminate sentence up to 3 years; only served 9 months and was praised by Assistant D.A. O'Connor for his cooperation
Jackie Goldsmith	fixer/former LIU player	sentenced to 2 1/2 to 4 years
Irving Schwartzberg	fixer	sentenced to one year by Judge Barrett
Benjamin Schwartzberg	fixer	sentenced to one year by Judge Barrett
Cornelius Kelleher	fixer	sentenced to one year by Judge Barrett
Joe Benitende	gambler	sentenced to 4 to 7 years
Jack West	fixer	sentenced to 2 to 3 years
Nick Englises	gambler	given an indeterminate sentence of up to 3 years
Tony Englises	gambler	sentenced to 6 months
Eli Klukosky	fixer	suffered fatal heart attack while awaiting his trial.

Some significant sports scandals....

Arizona State, 1997: Two players plead guilty to point shaving; the inquiry, dating back to games in 1994, shows that 15 of 22 fraternities turned up in records of illegal gambling ring on campus.

Boston College, 1996: Thirteen football players are suspended for gambling on games; two players are found to have bet against their own team.

Maryland, 1995: Five athletes, including the starting quarterback on the football team, are suspended for gambling on sports.

Northwestern, 1994: Two players, one a starting tailback on the football team and the other a starting guard on the basketball team, are suspended for betting on college games.

Bryant College, 1992: Five basketball players, who had built up $54,000 in gambling debts, are suspended and a former player and student was arrested and charged with bookmaking.

Maine, 1992: Thirteen baseball players and six football players are suspended for gambling on games.

Florida, 1989: Four football players, including star-QB-to-be Shane Matthews, then a redshirt freshman, are suspended for betting on football games.

1947-1950: Thirty-two players at seven schools are implicated in a plot to fix 86 games. Included in the scandal are players from City College of New York and Kentucky.

Here are some other major point-shaving investigations:

1959-61: Thirty-seven players from 22 schools are implicated in point-shaving scandals (big names involved: Connie Hawkins and Jack Molinas).

1978-79: Organized crime figure Henry Hill and New York gambler Richard (The Fixer) Perry mastermind a scheme to fix nine Boston College games in concert with BC players Ernie Cobb, Rick Kuhn and Jim Sweeney. Kuhn, the only player convicted, serves two and a half years in prison for conspiracy to commit sports bribery and interstate gambling.

1984-85: Four Tulane starters, including John "Hot Rod" Williams, and one reserve are accused of shaving points in two games. Two of the five players, Clyde Eads and Jon Johnson, are granted immunity and testify that the others also shaved points in exchange for cash and cocaine. Williams was acquitted and none of the players did jail time but the university shut down the program until the 1989-90 season.

Made in the USA
Lexington, KY
13 January 2015